Th

From Hilbre to Snowdonia

Pete Evans

Gwasg Carreg Gwalch

First published in 2021
© text: Pete Evans
© photos: Sophia and Pete Evans

ISBN: 978-1-84524-397-5
Cover design: Eleri Owen

Published by Gwasg Carreg Gwalch,
12 Iard yr Orsaf, Llanrwst, Wales LL26 0EH
tel: 01492 642031
email: books@carreg-gwalch.cymru
website: www.carreg-gwalch.cymru

ACKNOWLEDGEMENTS

Many thanks to the following, who have helped in many ways in the writing of this book,

Cheshire Archives and local studies.

Gary Austin, former production manager at Welsh Water.

Peter Read, writer, poet and playwright.

The Quay Watermen's Association, particularly Celia Drew and Keith.

The many hard-working rangers and other staff in countryside services across the length of the river.

Sophia Evans, anchor of well-being, provider of encouragement, tea, and all of the good photographs.

Many thanks also to David Rowe and Greg Lovelock for assistance in preparation of the text.

Apologies to the many others who I am sure to have missed. Please note that despite the good work of others, I am fully responsible for the wild inaccuracies which will have eased their way in.

previous page: The Dee at Chester;
opposite: Flint Castle;
over: The Dee at Carrog

Contents

The Holy Dee

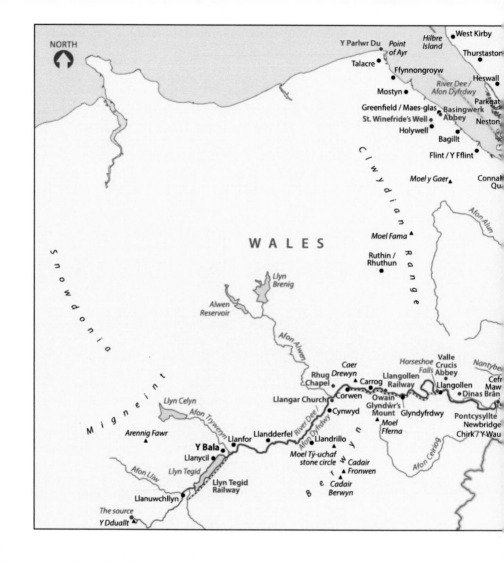

Burton
Steel works
Saughall
Shotton · Sealand · Chester
Queensferry · Blacon · Deva
Sandycroft · Point · Caerlleon
Hawarden Airport
Saltney · Roodee
Broughton · Huntington Water works
Eccleston
Eaton Hall
Aldford

ENGLAND

Almere
Farndon
Holt

Wrexham
Afon Clywedog
Shocklach Green

Bangor on Dee / Bangor-is-y-coed
Ruabon
Wynnstay Park · Overton Bridge · Erbistock · Manley Hall

MAELOR SAESNEG formerly FLINTSHIRE DETACHED

Llangollen Canal

0 miles 5
0 kilometres 10
Contains Ordnance Survey data
© Crown copyright and database right 2021

Preface

In a book covering the whole length of the Holy river, I have inevitably not included all the events and places where significant acts have occurred. I have noted the titles of many fine books which I have come across and can be referred to if I have sparked an interest for further reading, I'm sure there are many more. If you visit any of the places, then I hope you find as much interest and diversion and indeed joy as we have done over the last few years and will hopefully continue to find for a long time to come.

The walks were completed in a mixture of solo and partnered stages, where I use 'we' this refers to walks completed with Sophia unless otherwise stated.

To avoid spreading of non-native species, please follow good biosecurity practice. Follow the countryside code, respect the places, take away only memories, leave only footprints.

1. Introduction

John Aubrey in his Miscellanies of 1696 wrote:

"When any Christian is drowned in the river Dee, there will appear over the water where the corps is, a light, by which means they do find the body: and it is therefore called the Holy Dee".

THE MARITIME DEE

2. Where the tide meets the stream

The entrance to the Dee estuary with its shifting sands, where Snowdonia pours out her bounty, has long held navigational challenges for shipping. Hilbre Island had a light as far back as 1236, which the Earl of Chester paid annually for its upkeep. In medieval times Chester had grown into an important port, trading with the French wine ports, Dublin, and the boroughs of the North Wales coast, while in later years the Parkgate to Dublin packet route flourished. In the year preceding the building of Talacre lighthouse in 1776 the Irish Sea packets Nonpareil and the Trevor were both lost.

Talacre lighthouse originally housed two lights to guide ships entering the estuary, one shone toward Llandudno and one up the estuary, it was over 60 feet high, her lights were visible for nine miles in clear weather but they by no means brought an end to the dangers, in 1806 the packet ship King George was stranded on a sandbank with the loss of at least 106 souls.

Decommissioned in the 1880s, the lighthouse was replaced by a light ship. In 2010 she got a new keeper in the shape of a seven-foot-tall stainless-steel sculpture on the balcony, said to represent the figure of a ghost which haunts the building. Unlike the ghost, the residency of the artwork needed planning permission, for which a three-year period was granted.

And so it was that ten years almost to the day since we set off on our walk on the river Alun, we embarked on a similar journey along the Dee. As we walked toward the beach and the lighthouse appeared over the sand, we simultaneously reached for our cameras, turning our backs to the wind to keep rain off the lenses. The wind rose dramatically, spots of rain hit us hard. We dropped back down into the shelter of the natterjack-

Talacre Light House

dunes, until the rain eased off sufficiently for us to leave the semi-shelter into the buffeting unconstrained wind squalls; white Lawrence of Arabia sand blew in lines along the long beach from the direction of Prestatyn. The Wirral was a smudge of grey, under whiter shades of pale, Turner skies. The lighthouse was, some years ago, made over for a paint commercial. That paint is long gone, patches of bare scratch-coat plaster are exposed. Old photos show the dunes extending around the lighthouse, which today sits aloof on the point. I went to the seaward side to take a photo with the vast expanse of beach running into the Dee estuary in the background, meeting Sophia on the landward side where she was attempting shots with windblown streaks of sand over the steps "Is it me or is it on an angle?" I'd had a similar thought seconds earlier but put it down to me leaning into the wind, but yes, re-examined, the lighthouse appeared to sit on a huge, upturned saucer of concrete, which must be prone to eroding sands beneath her, there were no visible signs of the original oak pile foundations.

The sand dunes once stretched from here along the coast to Rhuddlan. During the Second World War the warren area of the dunes served two conflicting purposes. Evacuees seeking refuge from the bombing of Liverpool set up home here, in chalets, an old bus, and a railway carriage, while nearby, targets were erected for the use of spitfires which flew up the estuary from Hawarden. The last of the chalets was cleared in the 1970s. The area is now designated a site of special scientific interest. Several years ago, we joined an atmospheric guided night-time walk here in search of Natterjack toads, which filled the air with a cacophony of croaks.

Interpretation boards gave details of wind farms, gas platforms and landmarks on the Wirral. Blackpool tower was pointed at 32 miles away, but these points were white-grey mysteries on this day. A skylark rose and was promptly blown sideways. My map aptly identifies the stretch of wind sheared water adjacent to the point as "Wild road."

The path took us east past salt marshes where a little egret's broad white wings suspended a narrow leg-trailing body, as it fell into a mud-lined channel. We walked toward Ffynnongroyw along the miner's path, past the orange flared but otherwise battle-ship grey terminal which receives gas from the offshore Celtic field to supply Connah's Quay power station via an underground pipe.

We paused at a bird hide where we were treated to the sight of a curlew, spearing, and probing the soft mud with its long down-turned beak. Lapwings played and tumbled, flashing black and white while in the distance, shelduck were equi-spaced on the mud, each claiming their own socially distanced territory.

Rounding a misty bend in the path we saw the outline of a man with a horse, drawing nearer, we could see it was a wooden sculpture of a miner feeding an apple to a pit horse, complete with a trailer of coal. Goldfinches flitted between seed head weeds at the old colliery, the buildings of which have been reduced to slab level. The first shaft was sunk here in the 1860s, it was one of the last deep coal mines to operate in Wales, closing in 1996. Mining in my mind has always been tough, the coalfield here extended under the Irish Sea, this was not a job for the claustrophobic. The Welsh name of Point of Ayr is Parlwr-du or black parlour, said to have been so-named by miners who transferred here and were pleased to find that the coal seams were thick enough to allow the luxury of allowing them to be worked while stood upright, compared to their previous crawling in the narrower seams of the Bettisfield collieries. With improved roof bolting, Point of Ayr was regarded as a 'safe pit,' though that term must be taken in the context of an extremely dangerous means of putting food on the table.

Hilbre Island emerged from subsuming mist; middle eye trailing behind her. A winding gear monument sits on the edge of the old colliery site with a backdrop of the gas terminal. The colliery employed around 800 at its peak in the 1950s, I'm guessing that out of office hours today the gas plant is run by a handful of staff. From coal to gas and wind turbines, cleaner and safer jobs for fewer workers.

The old wharf from where coal was shipped stands quiet, it is now lined with funky art panels depicting industries past and present. A local dog walker stopped to chat. He had spotted two figures way out on the sands which we had not noticed. "They want to be careful there". I asked if they were cockling. "No, not on a Sunday, and too far out anyway, it would be difficult to lug them back from there." He surveyed the area they were in, "They'll be all right if they stick on that sandbank but need to have their wits about them, the tide comes in like a racehorse out there, you can get distracted and before you know it you're up to your ankles in foaming seawater." He went on to tell us of how he was out cockling once, when an axle broke on their trailer. As the tide came in, they were forced to pile up the bags of cockles to stop the waters washing them away and run for the shore. He did not look the type to be easily scared, but his voice recalled a dangerous situation. He mentioned people trying to cross from here to get to the Wirral, not realising the channels can be 50 feet deep.

We crossed the gutter fawr, following the Wales Coastal Path (WCP) in warm sunshine. The raised embankment of an old railway line carried us through the reclaimed marsh where cows grazed, a

buzzard swooped low, the black aquiline tip of her yellow beak and mayor-chain of lighter chest feathers visible. Flashing red and yellow goldfinches tinkled, an immaculate white little egret flew over us with seemingly afterthought legs trailing behind.

The views were much better on day two as we walked toward Mostyn docks, jutting out into the estuary like the roots of a great oak searching for water. Hilbre Point, the eastern jaw of the estuary,

Pit pony sculpture, Point of Ayr

clearly visible four and a half miles away on the north west corner of Cheshire was a tantalising destination for later in our journey but for today we were leaving Point of Ayr to begin the walk along the fifteen miles of the western side of the estuary. Crossing the coast road, the WCP brought us to the relocated No. 2 pit winding gear, an interpretation board showed a photo of the gear in a busy dockside scene where we had stood some half an hour before.

Ffynnongroyw is a long linear settlement with lovely old miner's cottages. It was Sunday morning quiet though sadly many of the churches and chapels and businesses which served the village are no longer open. We came to a wooden signpost which guided us to the clear well which gives the village its name, a grill over the well spelled out the name beneath large stone slabs. The flow of water was modest. A photo of the church outside the village hall taken before piped water arrived in the 1920s showed two girls carrying buckets of water. The mining display mentioned that baths weren't put in the colliery until 1957, prior to that the miners went home 'in the black,' soaked in sweat, and washed at home in a tin bath in front of the fire. The miner's wives are said to have been, understandably so, very pleased when the baths were opened. The line of houses follows the shoreline, but the estuary cannot be seen due to the cob, which protects and divides.

At the southerly end of the village a foot bridge going over the railway line gave fantastic views up the estuary and out to sea. I could see a large irregular dark patch on the sand and said to Sophia "It's almost like a tight packed bunch of birds" "That's 'cos it is". I looked closer and they were indeed birds. "Are they knot?" I asked she who has better eyes than me, but she thought I had gone into Shakespearean speak. Closer inspection identified them as black tailed godwits.

A clear stream, partially fed no doubt by the clear waters of the well, flowed nearby. Cockle and mussel shells formed banks which crunched underfoot, a hitching post was just offshore, a cold wind blew from the north. Steep hills squeezed the WCP on to the road, which, along with the railway line sits tight between hill and shore. Thomas Pennant, in A Tour of Wales in 1773 wrote of this area how 'the land rises suddenly from the shore in fine inequalities, clayey, and plenteous in corn and grass, for two, three or four miles... the lower part is divided by picturesque dingles, which run from the mountains, and open to the sea, filled with oaks. The inferior parts abound with coal and freestone; the upper with minerals of lead and calamine, and immense strata of limestone and chert. The principal trade of the country is mining and smelting.'

Opposite Mostyn docks stands the

Lletty Hotel, with its carving of the honest man and a date of 1699 on the lintel above the door, the story goes that when the hotel was being built the owner had to suddenly return to his home, but left money behind to ensure that none of the tradesmen were out of pocket. "Lletty" means hotel or inn, which would make it "Hotel Hotel", Pendle Hill, not too far distant, manages to go one further in the repetition found within the designation, deriving from the Celtic *pen*, Old English *hul* and the additional *hill* to give Hill-Hill Hill. No matter how many times the name is said, the doors are sadly closed, seemingly in perpetuity.

Over the road I am pleased to relate there was lots of activity, a large chemical plant operates here, there is servicing of the offshore windfarm, and lots of train equipment was being worked on.

Mostyn has played an important role at several significant times in our history, Henry Bolingbroke (later Henry IV) is said to have disembarked at the quay in 1399 before seizing the crown from Richard II at Flint castle.

The Mostyn Estates website quotes a legend that Henry Tudor was forced to escape through a window at Mostyn Hall still known as the 'King's Hole' after a party loyal to the reigning King Richard III had arrived to apprehend him. It goes on to say that it was more likely to be his uncle and key founder of the Tudor dynasty, Jasper, who then went on to complete his escape by sailing from Mostyn Dock among a load of straw. Henry would go on to be victorious at Bosworth in 1485 and claim the throne. A window which played a notable role in history.

South of the docks we entered a wood, light and airy due to the bark of birch trees and the white aggregate path which twisted pleasingly through the trees. This is a new section of the WCP and a particularly fine one. We emerged at a gorgeous viewpoint surrounded by dressed stone blocks overlooking the beach which sits alongside the industrial areas. The river channel on this side coils around the industrial promontory. Mostyn has a long history of industry, coal was mined here from medieval times until the last mine suffered terminal flooding in the late 1800s, while the iron works closed in

1. The Honest Man, Mostyn;
2. Business and pleasure at Mostyn

1965. Hard industries claiming many lives. Plans have been unveiled for a tidal lagoon between Mostyn and Point of Ayr to harness the power of the tides and produce low carbon electricity, a new era may be about to begin. A lone fisherman nearby reeled in a small fish which he returned to the water to grow and fight another day.

A rough wall of grey stone blocks interspersed with yellow and red sandstone fringes the track which runs along the estuary, with ploughed fields to landward.

The tide was racing in now, birds concentrated in small clusters on their island sandbanks, for as long as they could, before they twisted and flashed upward away from the rising waters. "BAIT" and a phone number written on a stone block brought a smile to our faces, an opportunist entrepreneur was ready to supply the lonely fishermen.

The track leads to the Duke of Lancaster, also known as the Funship, at Llanerch-y-mor. At first view she seems to rise out of a field, as if having been carried to her resting place by a tsunami and left in a dribble of water perpendicular to the estuary.

The Duke of Lancaster was built in 1956 by Harland and Wolff in Belfast, at the same shipyard as the Titanic and is listed in the National Historic Ships register. In a time of silver service, with luxurious first-class cabins and state rooms, she mainly operated on the Heysham to Belfast route. The rise of the motor car was the death knell for passenger only ferries on the Irish Sea, in 1970 she was converted to a car ferry, operating until 1978 when she was laid up at Barrow in Furness, before passing into private ownership the following year and being beached here to be turned into a leisure and retail complex. The Funship era however was another short-lived episode in the life of this fascinating vessel.

We stood near her bow, admiring her sleek lines, and imagining the chink of glasses from within the ghost ship, a sad end. Maybe one day she'll break free to cross the Irish Sea for one last adventure.

As I drove past Holywell to complete the next section of the walk, I looked over the Dee, the low cloud made it hard to see where sea became land and land became sky. A liminal landscape, where sky sat above mist, above water, above shifting sands, above mud and stone. A stormy day followed, heavy squalls came in off the open sea across seams of tide and current, rain ran off my waterproof coat onto my inappropriately denimed legs as I resumed my walk at Llanerch-y-mor. The fast-flowing brown land water in the gutter was held up by the clearer salt water of the high tide. I said goodbye to The Duke of Lancaster who had more dignity with water lapping around her.

The sea was hitting the defensive wall, I could see where the surrounding grass had been flattened by waves on the previous tide, prominent signs advised of an alternative high-water tide route. I surveyed the course ahead, noting that there were spur paths leading inland at intervals, I proceeded with caution, keeping a weather eye open. A pair of curlews flew up in front of me, gulls surfed the stiff wind, oystercatchers probed the soft mud on the landward side, business as usual for the birds.

At Greenfield dock, the tide had raised the fishing boats onto the walls of the mud-canyon basin. There are some excellent interpretation boards here, a splendid feature of the coastal path, one of them is titled 'A Heyday at the expense of Slaves (1757-1807).'

"Greenfield Dock itself was constructed on a natural harbour in the early 1700s. Originally the dock had two wharfs protected by a breakwater. Raw copper from Parys Mountain on Anglesey was unloaded here and sent to Greenfield Valleys' mills to be turned into copper goods. The owners of Greenfield Valley

The Duke of Lancaster

and the dock grew rich and successful exporting these cups, pots, and manilas (a horseshoe shaped bracelet used as a form of currency) to the slave-trader ships in Liverpool to take to West Africa. Copper nails and sheets were used to sheath the hulls of ships sailing to the tropics to protect against a timber-eating 'shipworm' – the cause of many shipwrecks. Cotton bales that had been exchanged for slaves in the Americas were imported back here for spinning at Greenfield Cotton Mill, completing this infamous 'Triangular Trade' which was abolished in 1807." My hometown is Amlwch, the port near Parys

Mountain where the raw copper came from. My grandfather, Twm tŷ maen, was raised in a rough stone house on the slopes of the mountain.

Another board shows cockling on the Dee, their life cycle and how they are caught, it informs that the season lasts from July to December. Fifty licensed cocklers are permitted to take 300kg per day. On the opposite side of the harbour there is a statue of a large wooden cockle. Detritus from an unofficial firework party from the previous evening, left on dockside, blew in the melancholy breeze.

I thought back to the early 1980s when I used to pass here on the Friday evening train taking me home. I remember seeing heavy plastic curtains flapping in the wind in derelict buildings close to the railway line, possibly it was the recently closed Courtaulds site, I can't be sure; the excitement of seeing friends and family and the lure of the mind-clearing spaces of the sea-cliffs occupied the greater part of my thoughts.

The final section of Wat's Dyke runs along the side of the valley here to form a clear territorial marker. It is thought the Dyke was built between 1200 and 1600 years ago and is a reminder we are in the border lands, the marches, y gororau.

Long before the tragic slave trade association, Greenfield Dock had a much happier role to play in receiving pilgrims en-route to St. Winefride's Well. I decided to make a side visit, a mini pilgrimage, to the well. On a low tide, cockle shells flashed white in the stream entering the dock, sadly, although in season, there were no cockles on sale. I looked at the setting I was in, on the banks of a beautiful estuary, with the smell of sea in the air and listened to the glorious silence. I imagined this spot to be relocated on the Bay of Biscay with a choice of seafood sellers, rustic and swish offering the cockles, along with mussels, scallops and my own favourite, razor clams. I thought back to our camper van journeys along the north coast of Spain and remembered enjoying a fantastic plate of clams, which were translated on the menu as "Clams to the sailor's blouse", the taste transcended any words, in any language. Snapping out of my reverie, the road took me over the railway line and into the Greenfield Valley, an interpretation board with a colourful map introduces it as 'one and a half miles of woodland, reservoirs, ancient monuments and industrial history'.

At the lower end of the valley stand the light-stoned ruins of Basingwerk Abbey, where the bases of pillars peep through the grass as if they have been cut down with a giant scythe. Part of a network of Cistercian settlements that once dotted Wales, the oldest part of the abbey is the 12th-century chapter house, with the remains of the benches where monks sat for daily readings. Probably founded in 1131 by Ranulph earl of Chester, a board tells its golden age was from 1481 to 1523

when it was a centre of high culture under Abbot Thomas Pennant whose praises were sung by Welsh poets. A local legend tells of how a 12th century monk wandered into a local woodland attracted by a nightingale's song. He listened, enchanted for a short while, or so he thought. Returning to the abbey he discovered that many centuries had passed, and the abbey was in ruins. The monk then crumbled to dust. The monks had charge of St. Winefride's well until Henry VIII dissolved the abbey in 1536, more dust. We shall come across the Cistercians again on our journey along the Dee.

Basingwerk Abbey

Basingwerk is still a significant religious site. At the entrance to the nearby museum a fantastic mural marks the start of the 134-mile North Wales Pilgrim's Way to Bardsey Island, the 'land of 20,000 saints'. The mural gives a great overview on the delights on the way there, through woodland, over moors, taking in ancient churches.

The museum includes a re-built 19th century upland farmhouse from the slopes of Moel Famau and a dairy, as well as vivid interpretations of the valleys significant part in the industrial revolution. I see the agreeable sight of an engraving of the entrance to Amlwch harbour, where in a previous life, I kept a boat.

A path leads up the valley on the bed of the old Holywell railway line which was the steepest conventional railway line in Britain. Originally built for industry, it later changed to passenger use and carried many pilgrims up the valley before closing in the 1950s. It passes the pools which once powered the mills which processed cotton, paper, and various metals as well as corn but now stand quiet, one pool is a haven for fishermen.

I walked along a broad path in a tunnel of green, in silent drizzle. Yellow arrows and pilgrim's way signs reminded me of the final stages of our own pilgrimage along the Camino through Galicia to Santiago de Compostela. A fitting way to arrive at St. Winefride's, where the height of the buildings was accentuated by the steep slope of the upper valley.

J.S. Howson, Dean of Chester, and Alfred Rimmer (for brevity referred to as J.S. Howson only in subsequent text) in their book 'The River Dee its aspect and history' from 1892 described the feeling which lingers at St. Winefride's as "half-poetical, half-superstitious". I wouldn't disagree with that; I lit a candle which illuminated the small dark chapel and took the waters from the pump on the wall. In the shrine the clear waters flume out of the ground. A truly peaceful spot. On the 5th of January 1917, the flow was interrupted when, deep underground, workers digging the Milwr Tunnel, a 10-mile de-watering route from the lead mines in the Loggerheads area to the coast, broke into a flooded passage, releasing a huge outflow of water and depriving the well of its source. The flow was thankfully re-instated by diverting water from an area of old mine workings to the north-west of Holywell, restoring the healing waters and the peace. An interpretation board informs that the grade 1 listed building was built at the beginning of the 16th century and that this sophisticated and beautiful building is a gem of late perpendicular architecture and is unique in the world. The well has been a place of pilgrimage for over 1300 years.

How it came to be and survived through the dissolution and penal laws is an incredible story, told in the museum, where a collection of the redundant crutches of the healed can be seen.

Continuing my walk along the coast I saw cows grazing on the salt marshes and the last rays of the sun catching the old Mostyn school in Parkgate. Deeside industrial estate was in a bubble of cloudless sky surrounded by storm clouds.

Charles Kingsley, when he was the Canon of Chester Cathedral, wrote 'The Sands of Dee' after hearing the tale of a young woman who had been lost on the Dee marshes, the first two verses give a vivid account of the dangers.

'O Mary, go and call the cattle home,
And call the cattle home,
And call the cattle home,
Across the sands o' Dee;'
The western wind was wild and dank
    wi' foam,
And all alone went she.

The creeping tide came up along the
    sand,
And o'er and o'er the sand,
And round and round the sand,
As far as eye could see;
The blinding mist came down and hid
    the land—
And never home came she.

I arrived at "The Holy", the local name for the outfall of the Milwr tunnel, at Bettisfield. It was clear the tide has turned, sandbanks were visible toward the Wirral side, the unhindered Dee powered around the base of the cob, brown and full of nutrients for the cockles and waders. At the colliery site, the old winding house is now within a scrap yard, a metal figure of a man stands in one of the windows, one of several artworks nearby. I wondered if he is on a job timeshare between here and the lighthouse at Talacre. Rounding the headland at Bettisfield, the Dee lapped against the rocks making a very soothing noise which prompted me to pause and take in the views of the wide-open estuary under the high skies.

At Bagillt (Station Gutter), a plaque commemorates the station which stood there. Being not up to speed with the current rail line provisions, I had briefly considered taking a train back to my car at the end of the days walk, but the plaque firmly ruled out that possibility, informing me that the station closed in 1966. I have been late for a few trains over the years, but this was a new record.

Sheep and a few cows grazed on fertile undulating fields protected by the

1. St. Winefride's Well;
2. Bettisfield Warrior, his shield shows the four choughs representing Flintshire

embankment on which I walked. The path was uneven, I noticed another lower down which was straight and even and nearer the water. Wispy clouds of bird's smoke rose above the water, geese honked.

A man, 72 years to heaven, stopped to chat, he was from Flint which I could see in the distance, he told me he walks two to three miles a day in this area, preferring winter to summer, which he finds "too hot, with too many children around". He pointed to a buoy about 50 feet out in the water and told me when he was a lad the shoreline would have extended past it. As I had walked on the lower path, I could see the bank was being eroded away, chunks of clay-like soil falling onto the rocks, a little further on the lower-level path tapered to nothing. He pointed out the grassy marshland further out into the estuary, extending much further across from Wirral than it used to, a dynamic estuary. An O.S. map dated 1927 confirms the main channel of the Dee at that time turning out from Flint to the Wirral coast at Heswall and Thurstaston.

Curlew and Little Egrets

Nearing Flint, I came to a group of six eastern European fishermen on the embankment who were reeling in lots of whiting. One of them told me he enjoyed fishing but did not eat fish himself, giving his catch to his wife and mother-in-law, which seemed like a good deal to me for an afternoon's fishing at this lovely spot. Flint dock is mostly silted up but much bigger than the previous gulley's. On a receding tide, two curlews swooped and called their beautifully haunting whistle-warble.

Flint Dock

In contrast, a pair of little egrets cawed at each other as they argued over the best fishing point where the waters lapped the rocks, a gull sometimes becoming embroiled in the argument. The egrets call does not tie up with their whiter than white appearance. A cormorant (bilidowcar) sat on the exposed sand and stretched out its wings to dry in the wind, looking like a medieval flag. A great crested grebe glided past. A magical spot for birds, right in front of the dock.

Flint castle is in an imposing position on the Dee estuary, able to control the river traffic and the historic fording point to the Wirral.

In 1277, Edward I gathered a massive army in Chester and marched into Wales to fight Llywelyn ap Grufydd, Prince of Gwynedd, who had refused to pay homage to him on his return from the crusades. He consolidated his victory by building the castle, a fortress easily supplied by sea which was largely complete by 1284. It was given the name 'Le Flynt' and would have been lime washed white to add to its formidable appearance on the hard-rocky ground at the edge of the marshy estuary.

The earliest and most unusual of Edward I's castles, 10,000 blocks of sandstone for the foundations were brought across from the Wirral on 250 rafts. The military architecture is unique and unusually sophisticated, following designs Edward had seen in France, it is dominated by the great tower (or donjon) at its south-east corner. Surrounded by its own moat and accessed via a drawbridge, it is essentially a castle within a castle. Built with exceptionally thick walls and equipped with all the facilities required to withstand a siege, it was presumably intended to be a final refuge in the event of an attack. The castle was indeed attacked on several occasions, it was besieged even before building was complete and again by supporters of Owain Glyndŵr from 1400 to 1403.

Flint was a 'bastide' a planned new town, the first of many English-only colonies and was a launchpad for Edward I's further military operations which would be a huge undertaking, possibly the biggest building project in medieval Europe, Thousands of woodcutters, builders and dykers were drafted in from as far away as the Fens and Holland to build his castle towns across North Wales.

In 1399 Richard II surrendered here to Henry Bolingbroke, the second Duke of Lancaster we have encountered on this coastline, who became Henry IV. A plaque tells the story of how Richard's faithful dog Mathe deserted him, choosing to follow Bolingbroke, apparently loyal to the crown and not him.

During the Civil War, the castle was garrisoned by royalist supporters in 1642 who fought against Oliver Cromwell's forces. Despite being reinforced from Ireland by troops who landed at Mostyn, it fell to parliamentary forces and was largely destroyed sometime after 1646.

I thought about the many past conflicts here as I gained easy free access via the metal walkway which extends from a stone pier over the deep dyke, walking past the formidable remains of the grand tower on my right. New arched-iron security gates at the entrance and leading to the North-Eastern tower nicely follow the lines of the castle into the historic stones.

Turner visited Flint on all three of his tours through north Wales, his 1835 watercolour of the castle is one of his greatest Welsh landscapes. He captured a working seascape with ships being unloaded in swirling morning mist and shrimpers in the foreground under a heavenly watery sunrise.

A modern-day battle was recently played out here, when plans for a ring of steel sculpture divided opinion. It is a great spot for a large sculpture, I hope the final design sympathetically reflects all the blood and tears which have fallen here. For me, as I look back at the castle from the WCP, I reflect that the greatest monument may have already been built. The 870-mile-long path which opened in 2012 is a fantastic achievement, we are the first country in the world to have a footpath hugging our entire coastline. For those who walk the entire path and have strength remaining in their legs, they can continue to walk along the 177 miles of the Offa's' Dyke Path making a circuit of Wales through the borders. From being ringed by castles, although they are undoubtedly beautiful, they were built as a means of control, to a circle of footpaths designed for freedom, what a fantastic forward-thinking statement.

I take my hat off to the people who made the WCP possible and continue to work to keep it open. Industrial

A King's best friend

Flint Castle

The Holy Dee

development had closed off or caused some historical routes along the coast to be lost, there was degraded land, fly-tipping, and uncontrolled use by motorcyclists. Access had to be maintained for fishermen and farmers within legal boundaries and protected natural sites, and of course funding had to be found. Access to the WCP is free, no membership is required, there is no dress code or expensive equipment required, we are all auto enrolled to walk here just by the very fact of being alive. To enjoy it with friends or alone when space and mental disentanglement is required is something to be celebrated to the skies.

Onward to Oakenholt marshes, where oystercatchers peeped and dipped in and out of the gulley's looking for cockles and mussels, alive, alive-o in one of the best wader sites in Europe. I turned inland toward the main road and noticed doggy doo on my left boot, I did my best to clean the unwelcome hitchhiker away, but by the time I got to the main road, there was a leaf covered pancake beneath my right boot, both feet right in it.

At the southern end of Oakenholt marshes is the Deeside Naturalist's Society reserve. It is a terrific location, a fantastic refuge sitting next to the power station, yet which is very relaxing. A place of sunshine and storms, of kingfishers and waders.

Arriving at the Flintshire bridge, I was aware that this is a point of much significance, the fulcrum of the estuary, the first bridge I would come to and the newest crossing point on the Dee, opened in 1998, she is the largest asymmetric cable-stayed bridge in the whole of Britain and a real beauty. Before continuing upstream, the joys of the eastern shores of the estuary beckoned us, we were helpless to resist.

3. The Wirral – Cilgwri – Land of Ouzels – England – Lloegr – Cheshire

Sadly, it's not possible to cross the Flintshire Bridge on foot. We deployed our bicycles at Dock Road in Connah's Quay and set off. Shortly before Hawarden railway bridge, we stopped to chat to a man whose Labrador was romping in the riverside pools which had been left by the high tides of a few days previous. He told us his dog sometimes retrieves stranded salmon and fluke, though he was keen to emphasise that he never keeps them and that he gets all his fish from Iceland (the shop).

Brown late winter meltwaters flowed beneath the bridge as we crossed into the Deeside Industrial Park. Leaving National Cycle Route number 5 after travelling a very modest section of its 381 miles from Reading to Holyhead, we joined the much shorter Route number 568, also known as the Burton Marsh Greenway, which runs from Hawarden Bridge to Neston, where a connection can be made to the Wirral Way. There seems to be an improvement in cycleways now which is very pleasing, it's a few years since I cycled to work on the roads, an experience which could at times be 'a bit hairy', compared to my experiences of cycling in Germany in the 1980s, which was on dedicated and safe cycle lanes. We pressed on, adjacent to the railway line through some open country with a smallholding and bird boxes, before reaching the industrial units. We saw beehives on a patch of land between units and a field of solar panels under which rabbit's twitched, a multi-purpose area.

We passed the factories, many signed with familiar company names, their locations now revealed to us, before leaving the industry behind and going by the Sealand Rifle Range which was all quiet. I attended a guided walk here, with an unlikely and very welcome alliance of representatives of the MOD, Tata Steel, Flintshire rangers, the RSPB and Dee Wildfowlers, a fantastic range of

From Wales to England, Flintshire to Cheshire onto the Wirral peninsula – Cilgwri.

knowledge made for an interesting visit.

Over the years the range has been used for all manner of target practice including with tanks and aerial firing. Today it is used by the army and police as well as civilian clubs for the firing of small arms. We were guided to the top of a protective bank from which we had great views of the expanse of the estuary. The marshes here have a language of their own, Polwalla gutter, flash, and knobs (a high point), extended in front of us, there was Smiths Flash, Flash beyond Smiths, and Sandlulls Flashes each with their own local knowledge gathered over the years. In the re-claimed area we were in, water continues to be pumped out at high tide over the Broken Bank (named after a historic breach).

Teal, pintail, black tailed godwits, redshank, widgeon, mallard, stonechat, water rail, and reed warbler can all be found in the estuary as well as pinkfoot, canada and greylag geese, these also have

their own language, drifting in whistles, calls and shrieks over the marsh. Up to 90% of the estuary dries out at low water spring tides, forming the fifth largest intertidal flats within an estuary in the UK. Up to 3,000 sheep, producing premium Saltmarsh Lamb, graze on the marshes, from which they need to be brought in on high tides. A tough environment to farm, the landscape does not allow quadbikes, a lot of foot miles are required.

The Mabinogion, the collection of medieval Welsh tales based on mythology, folklore, and heroic legends, tells of the thirty-nine seemingly impossible tasks set by the father of the beautiful maiden Olwen for Culhwch to complete before he could take her hand in marriage.

One of the tasks was to find Mabon ap Modron who was taken from his mother when he was three nights old. Culhwch asks for the help of King Arthur who enlisted two men of his court, Cei and Bedwyr, as well as Gwrhir, who could speak with animals and birds.

They went on their way as far as the Ouzel of Cilgwri (Wirral), to ask if she could remember what happened to Mabon. She told her inquisitors of her great age but that she had heard aught of Mabon. She offered to guide them to an older animal than she, and so begins the cycle of the oldest and wisest animals, which we shall encounter more of on our journey along the Dee.

The path drops down to a lovely board-walked area across marshy reed beds in front of Burton point. Lazy curves of water channels flowed easily through the reed beds, which I scanned for water voles. We heard a curlew, saw a skein of geese overhead. Burton point was cloaked in a soft mist, like a Chinese watercolour painting in which delicate wispy trees shimmered in front of the green bank, which led the eye to the quarried straight vertical face of the red sandstone cliffs. I paused here on my bicycle on a warm day, some years ago, to listen to the gorse pods popping open to eject their seeds, flying ants prevented us from any lingering on this visit.

There are always smiles in Burton Mere RSPB reserve visitor centre around the wood burning stove and in front of the big windows with their fantastic views to the Clwydian hills. The scrapes and lagoons provide a valuable high-water refuge for the birds of the estuary.

From the hill within the reserve there are glorious views over the Dee marshes to the promontory at Little Ness, the old sea-less quay, and further to Parkgate, the hills of Thurstaston and Hilbre Island which seemed to hover above the sea. A deceit (blame Chaucer) of Lapwing flew just over our heads and then plunged as if hit by invisible snipers before they recovered control and landed.

Amongst the sycamores are the remains of an Iron Age fort, an artist's impression shows a 5-metre-high bank of earth and stone surrounded by a ditch with a couple of reed roofed houses within. The waters of the Dee are shown extending up to the base of the promontory with canoes on the water. The board goes on to explain how industry robbed many areas of their value to wildlife, but the RSPB has been giving back parts of the Dee estuary to nature since the 1980s. The wildlife has returned in such substantial numbers that the estuary is now one of the most highly protected wildlife sites in the UK.

The village of Burton is well worth a digression to appreciate the former fishermen's black and white cottages coasting on the sloping red sandstone. The clock face in the tower of the church, fittingly dedicated to St. Nicholas, the patron saint of mariners, has only an hour hand, made in a time when minutes were not as crucial as in our warp speed days.

From Puddington I previously joined an evening's "Wet walk into Wales" guided by the Dee wildfowlers and a coastal ranger. Walking out into the marshes, we used staffs to probe our way across the water channels into, for me, an unfamiliar terrain, a cryptic landscape of soft lulling grasses with searching tides. A rain shower came fast up the estuary, a beautiful rainbow formed over Burton Point, a flash of white wings turned under the arc, in front of black clouds.

Bright green spreading samphire, also known locally as sampkin grew out of the brown cracked mud, resembling small conifers as we crossed the boundary line shown on the map between Wirral and Flintshire into Wales. There are no boundary stones, signposts, or customs checks where seascape has become landscape, soil has replaced sand and water, and foxes now burrow.

Arriving at an area known to wildfowlers as Taylors Gutter, a name not on my map, we saw the bobbing black heads of Canada geese, herons, and a stilted egret. Oystercatchers flew hard along the muddy edges; the giddy calls of curlews claimed the sky above the estuary. Curved mounds of flotsam grass were speckled with the bleached white carcasses of crabs and seashells.

The wildfowlers told us of William Kemp, who earned a living fowling, salmon fishing and grazing on the saltings, spending more time on the water than on land so that he became known locally as 'Billy the Duck'. The club manage the marsh to attract and sustain wildfowl, controlling the herbage, and trying to control the ongoing siltation.

The walk back was under a huge blue sky, fringed by a great sunset over Flint which turned the sky pink, purple and orange. Skeins of pink footed geese flew back to their roosts. A wonderful full moon rose above us.

The sun broke through, we stopped at a café for a break before deciding to press on to Ness Point where we viewed the landlocked quayside, though a reedy, driftwood strandline deposited by the previous week's spring tides which showed that the sea is not a total stranger here. We leaned our bicycles against a tree and took in the expansive view, I saw what looked like a marsh harrier quartering in front of us, as it got closer, we could see the large head and the slow-motion action of long, elegant wings and realised it was a short-eared owl hunting right in front of us, sweeping low and dropping to reveal brilliant browns and whites and yellows on her upper wings, a treat indeed. She landed in front of us, yellow day-hunting eyes drilling into us before rising and then dropping to catch an unseen vole or some other unfortunate prey, but before she could eat her hard-earned meal, a kestrel swooped down from the tree behind us. There was a flurry of flapping wings and raised talons, the larger owl deciding to head off and leave the aggressive highwayman to his spoils. What a sight to witness. A second owl was sweeping the marshes in the distance, a smoking murmuration came closer, close enough to identify geese whiffling down on to the grass, a recent RSPB report mentioned there were three to four thousand pink footed and greylag geese on the estuary, who needs television?

A great white egret with its long white neck and orange bill extending above the grass like an avian periscope was a first for us, bigger than a nearby heron. Little egrets also provided flashes of white in the green-brown grass, we see them regularly now, though I vividly remember the excitement of my first sighting of one about fifteen years ago, a welcome addition to the songline of my knowledge.

Short Eared Owl

We heard the unmistakable rising and falling call of a curlew, much written about, it is said to trigger a range of emotions. For me it makes me smile, I can feel a breeze on my face, taste salt on my lips, I only experience the said melancholy of their song if I think of their plummeting numbers. Two short eared owls entertained us, quartering, and posing on posts, their heads swivelling in Linda Blair fashion. Stonechats and meadow pipits were the support act.

An interpretation board, commissioned by the Burton and Neston historical society in 2009, the 250th anniversary of the opening of the Neston collieries gives a vivid overview of the collieries. Almost all the coal was obtained from under the Dee estuary, the mines extended almost two miles under the river and were accessed by up to thirty shafts in the nearby area. There are records of children as young at nine years old working in the mine; they would have cost half of what a man earned. The village of Ness was described in 1847 as 'one of the most miserable in Wirral with a mass of hovels inhabited by the miners.' Some of them worked 100 hours a week including 16-hour shifts. There was a constant risk of accidents from falls into shafts, rock collapses, explosions, and poisonous gases.

The board shows a cutting headlined Chester Spring Assizes, which is dated April 1822 and deals with a case of trespass. The court found against Thomas Stanley, the mine owner, on two occasions, but this didn't stop his transgressions, he later used pumps in his own mine to deliberately flood the workings in the adjoining Little Neston colliery whose competition forced him to lower his prices.

It is little wonder they enjoyed a drink at the Harp Inn which still stands here. I procured a glass of bitter and sat on the grass bank outside, raised it to the sky in my office-soft hand and toasted the people who toiled and gave their lives beneath my feet.

Denhall Quay was built in 1791...but silting of the Dee gradually made boat access impossible – probably the main reason for Ness Colliery's eventual closure in 1855. A second interpretation board at the northern end of the village covers Neston's second phase of coal mining from 1874 to 1927 which was made possible by the coming of the railways. It is really well illustrated with a painting from 1875 and some great photos, including one of the area after the mine closed showing a large chimney which was due to be demolished as a public spectacle – but came down in a storm the night before its scheduled demise!

As the day gained on us, we chatted to a couple who were hoping to see a barn owl, they mentioned the numbers were down due to the wet weather in recent years which made it difficult for them to hunt. As we chatted, their wish was granted as he spotted one over our shoulders gliding silently, a dignified passing of soft browns and white about 100 yards distant over the marsh.

As the dusk set in we headed back towards Puddington, seeing the barn owl once more sitting nonchalantly on a 'danger military firing' sign. A row of orange and white lights marked the Welsh shore, the wind dropped along with the temperature, we heard ducks laughing, geese grumbling, diverse peeps and the fluting call of a curlew, the shriek of a pheasant. Our heartbeats slowed to the natural rhythm of the earth. Little egrets passed overhead, about eight or so single birds heading back to an unseen roost. As we approached the car along the lane, bats

swooped low almost in touching distance, the sky burned its way down behind the horizon, fingers of mist extended along the flanks of Moel Famau, swirls of pinks and blues and grey extended up into the half-moon vapour trail scratched sky.

In a morning's start from Little Ness, we squelched north on wet marsh grass, magnificent birdsong carried up into a high sky. Estuary walking has its own expansive feeling of deep breaths of fresh air. Underfoot the terrain turned to glorious mud as long-tailed tits, goldfinches and a greenfinch flitted in the hawthorns. We came to another atmospheric high and dry old sandstone quay, footbridges carried us over little brooks draining the sodden land of recent rains. There were bulrushes on our left, while coconut fragrant gorse was in bloom to our right. I felt my heartbeat slow and shoulders drop under a thousand-mile-high sky, whispering head height reeds with nodding flaxy ears led us to a wooden footbridge under a yellow mossy willow tree, a truly lovely spot kept quiet from best shoe promenaders by the deep mud.

Springwater was drawn up by a pump at a bend in the path which took us a short distance through a residential area before emerging at one of several slipways which lead into the marsh from Parkgate.

Parkgate has a gorgeous promenade with a pub at each end and a chip shop in the middle, all that is missing is the sea. But here's the thing – it doesn't matter. Families walk, pushing prams, children eat ice cream, cars are parked up with snoozing occupants. Keening gulls drop from the huge sky, the marshes give a lightness of salt air, the birds which rise

To the jaws of the estuary

above them are nature's free issue entertainment.

We stopped to enjoy a refreshing ice cream on the curved and worn sandstone wall which seldom sees the sea. At the centre of the promenade there are interpretation boards where a customs house stood until 1840. They tell us that Parkgate was an outport of Chester, particularly as a point of embarkation for Ireland and for ferry services to Bagillt and Flint. The Irish packet trade transferred to

Liverpool in 1815 due to silting of the river. As mentioned earlier, the route from Parkgate was a hazardous one,

> *Where were ye, Nymphs, when the*
> *   remorseless deep*
> *Clos'd o'er the head of your lov'd*
> *   Lycidas?*
> *For neither were ye playing on the steep*
> *Where your old bards, the famous*
> *   Druids, lie,*
> *Nor on the shaggy top of Mona high,*
> *Nor yet where Deva spreads her wizard*
> *   stream.*
> *Ay me! I fondly dream.*

So wrote John Milton in his poem Lycidas in memory of his friend Edward King who was lost when the packet he was on foundered, it is thought on the Anglesey coastline, on its way from Parkgate to Ireland around 1637.

Parkgate became well known as a bathing resort from the late 18th century until the 1930s, many came for the sea air and the water which were thought to have curative powers. The open-air baths were a great attraction from 1923 to 1950. Other snippets I glean from the boards are that the 10,000 acres of land reclaimed from the sea purchased by John Summers and Sons in 1896 included the marshes here which have been managed by the RSPB since 1979 and that Mostyn Hall near the port of Mostyn, shown on a map of the opposite shore, is the home of the family which owned most of Parkgate until 1849.

Black headed gulls tripped and shrieked around a pond, a male Hen harrier, black tipped wings patrolled behind them, not long now until he returns to his hafod in the summer hills. Our usual trips to Parkgate are by motorised means, squeezing down the promenade with numerous other seekers of a quasi-seaside resort. It was great to arrive on foot, to savour the full walk along the promenade, to stop at the plaques placed by Parkgate Historical society to celebrate the past. We circled St. Thomas' church, set back in Mostyn square, which was unfortunately closed. As we sat on a bench outside to take in the views across the estuary, we noted that there are three windowless arches above us, and pondered why? Possibly to protect against gales off the estuary, or to keep the minds of the parishioners from straying in the sermon to those lovely views?

If a strong wind pushes the equinoctial

spring tides, the waters can still reach the seawall. The old bath's car park is as good a spot as any to watch the drama unfold as birds are flushed out of the marshes and voles and other creatures scramble for safety while being pursued by avian predators. We have parked our trusty old campervan broadside to the wind here in winter gales, enjoying fish and chips, steaming hot mugs of tea and nature at its best. The best restaurant in the world.

As we left the honeypot that is Parkgate we saw a marsh harrier performing low sweeps over the reeds in which it flapped and glided, twisted, and dropped to investigate potential meals. The sky in the distance briefly looked pixilated as a mass of geese headed up the estuary. When I was younger, I thought I had to watch documentaries on far flung places, maybe the Camargue or the Serengeti to see such things.

From the raised pathway on the sandstone wall, we could see the runs of mice and voles through the reeds as we made our way to Gayton. Skylarks hung and sang their hearts out and were briefly visible high in the sky or seemingly crash landing into the ground. Their sound was interspersed with the occasional drive off

a golf ball at the adjacent Heswall Golf Club and ... the first time I had heard it for years ... a "Fore!" The only sand visible on this former shoreline was in the bunkers on the landward side. We leave Cheshire behind us and cross quietly into the Metropolitan Borough of Wirral. A ferry service once operated from Gayton Cottage to Greenfield, nowadays, a hefty portage would be required to reach the silvery sinews of water in the marshes. In 1690 King William III (William of Orange) stayed at nearby Gayton Hall while waiting for suitable weather to depart with his troops from Hoylake for Ireland and the Battle of the Boyne.

We arrived at the Riverbank Road car park in a very heavy rain shower, an idyllic spot with splendid views of the estuary over the slipway which leads into the marshes which could only be chanced upon by car if lost. As we walked through the reeds, the sea felt closer as we saw numerous mermaid's purses and the egg sacs of whelks, the views of the Welsh coast then softened before it disappeared completely. Rain and thick mud stopped play. At the end of our short walk a vehicle pulled up, the driver opened the tailgate, two large dogs spilled out and emptied their bowels with some gusto as he sat on a bench having a cigarette. If you do find yourself in this lovely spot, my advice would be to follow the words of the Monty Python crew on a mission through the sewers of a Roman palace in Life of Brian, "don't wear your best sandals".

We re-joined the coast a little way downstream at Banks Road. I breathed deeply of the now rich ozone full sea-salt air. We strolled past Heswall boat yard where boats were being made ready for the new season. Further along a sign advised "Warning – unstable cliffs keep away" while another "Deep mud – Do not walk out into the estuary." Not knowing if and where a suitable happy medium route lies between these two dangers and, due to the heavens now having opened, we retreated and found shelter under a boat on a trailer. We spent the next half hour watching the Welsh coast disappear completely and then briefly reappear to raise our hopes only for ever more torrential spells of rain to fall like stair rods. One hardy fisherman tried to carry on his knocking and scraping while putting a sack over his back, but he too eventually had to bid a retreat from the elements. We saw out the downpour's cheek by jowl with a barnacled bilge.

1. Parkgate; 2.Heswall

When the rain finally eased, we emerged for long enough to steal a photo and chat to a man readying his tender, who told us it is possible to launch from here within an hour either side of high tide and how boats still fish for shrimps. The slipway is straddled by two large anchors, one of which was caught in a trawl and took three men to raise it to allow it to be suspended from the bow to get it to shore.

The rain resumed; we passed the restaurant which we have been meaning to eat at for some time but have not managed to catch it open. On this occasion, it was, but it probably was not an appropriate time for two muddy-booted bedraggled and dripping souls to call in.

Nearing Thurstaston

We managed to get to Thurstaston Visitor Centre just before it closed and were the only guests. There was a bucket catching rainwater drips from a leak, reinforcing our thoughts that this was not a great day to be out walking. There was a

lovely illustration of 20 birds which are found on the estuary pleasingly titled "The Dee Estuary – Mud and Marsh."

A video played on a loop giving great views of Hilbre Island and of a large flock of dunlin over-wintering before returning to Africa for the summer. On the deserted, sodden cliffs nearby we disturbed a large flock of oystercatchers who flashed black and white and whistled and peeped as their orange-pointed beaks guided them up and away. We walked on to the Dee Sailing Club which whispered of sunny days to come, in its idyllic location above a rain washed and empty slipway, as halyards and downhauls tapped impatiently on sleeping masts.

It was a chilly night in the campervan, but we were rewarded with a beautiful dawn chorus as chinks of sunlight melted the ice off our windscreen. The various peeps and tweets were a full symphony including the percussion of a woodpecker on a nearby tree. We took a delightful early morning walk above the estuary which had an open low-tide, high blue-sky ambience as opposed to yesterday's high-tide low cloud, closed in feeling. Bright orange and blue fishing boats and buoys on golden sands traced the deep channels and chicanes. We could see the red funnel of the Funship highlighted on the Flintshire shore. A fellow early riser who had been at the site for a rain-lashed week asked for help in identifying "that strange bright thing in the sky". The campsite stirred itself into life, a boiling kettle whistled, the smell of toast and bacon filled the crisp morning air.

The Wirral Way was drying out, helped by numerous feet and tyres and hooves as we cycled to its end point at West Kirby. We stopped at Cubbins Green just before the town to take in more of those great views.

After negotiating a few busy streets, we emerged onto the seafront, which was alive with morning people and their dogs, shaking off the night, chattering in a human dawn chorus, breathing deep of the sea fresh air, and gratefully accepting the gift of sunshine. All was well with the world.

Arriving at the infinity pool marine lake, the largest in Europe, we saw a seaweed fronded wall, warning signs were placed against weaver fish, which bury themselves in the sand. An unlucky bare foot could stand on a spine delivering enough poison to require a hospital visit.

In the distance people were walking on water in a sea of Galilee style, dogs too, along the hidden path on the lakeside wall. Further again we could see a smattering of walkers making their way past Little Eye, one of them broke away, an escapee from the group, to stand statue like on top of it before speeding his way on to catch up with them. We pinpointed Talacre lighthouse, five miles away on the opposite shore closing the gaping jaws of the estuary and marking the point where we had started our walk some five months earlier.

The name West Kirby is Scandinavian in origin deriving from the Old Norse words kirkja (church) and byr (farm or settlement) meaning 'village with a church'. 'West' was added to differentiate it from Kirby in Wallea, the old name for Wallasey which has its origins in the Germanic word for foreigner, as does Wales.

A gentle breeze was blowing, forming white horses which raced behind Hilbre. We continued along the strand line, passing another golf course, our third in the last few days, a golf coast. The sandy beach led us on to a trail through marshes and popping reeds with dunes to the rear.

This is Cheshire Wildlife Trusts only coastal reserve, a SSSI and a fine one at that. In spring the rasping competitive calls of male natterjack toads can carry for up to a mile, luckily in this case, not far enough to tempt any females at Talacre to a watery grave. Razor shells peppered the shoreline, skylarks sang their hearts out high above us before plummeting in stages to perform a last-minute recovery and glide back low to their hidden nests.

A board outside the lifeboat station we passed earlier, in addition to giving times of high and low water, forecasted an air temperature of seven degrees centigrade, but in a sheltered arm of Hilbre Point families were picnicking and enjoying the sun in the last days of winters grasp. We looked back down the stretch of the estuary, seeing only sand, when we started our estuarine walk some twelve miles away, we could see only marsh, then only reeds, bringing us through mud and sand to here, where the Wirral slips into Liverpool Bay.

We have only walked to the estuary

1. The marine lake, where people walk on water; 2. Approaching West Kirby; 3. Early morning at Thurstaston

guarding safeness of Hilbre once, I remember the expanse of rippled and crab-pooled sands, a light-footed advancement across the littoral zone under a blue and white stroked sky which reached up to the heavens, the nose-tingling excitement of ozone. A contemporary evening walk with rangers had to be cancelled due to thunderstorms in the area, flat open sands not being a good place to be when lightening seeks the earth.

Our walk there had taken us up through the layers of red sandstone which are gradually being unpicked by the sea, onto the green grass top, the colours accentuated by the marine setting and the westering light. A single road traverses her back, servicing the surprising number of buildings, mostly along her eastern leeside, behind a grey sun-dried picket fence, though there are no permanent residents since 2011 when difficulties were encountered in finding a live-in custodian prepared to live without mains electricity or running water and being cut off from the mainland by the tides. Grey seals and migratory birds continue to make good use of this sanctuary staging post at the tip of the estuary.

A bird observatory, a ranger's building and the telegraph station sat among the white flagless poles, while at the northern end the old lifeboat station, enjoyed the summer days of her retirement, the layers of red sandstone washed up into her walls, the quiet sea was in a benevolent mood.

Hilbre, a sacred island in early times, is said to take its name from a medieval church dedicated to St. Hildeburgh, a cell of Benedictine monks was established here around the eleventh century and remained until the dissolution.

The half a mile or so of Hilbre does not stand alone. The oblique slash of weathered sandstone running away from the Wirral shore consists of three outcrops. The middle Eye (shown as Little Hilbre on my map) is half the size of her big sister, while further to the south east, Little Eye is smaller again. Having three islands in my mind qualifies the Hilbre Islands to be identified as an Archipelago, an exotic word which I was not expecting to come across in walking the Dee.

From the red rocks of Hilbre point we looked to the east to Hoylake lifeboat station and beyond it a miraged shore of

the eastern Irish Sea. We thought we could see a white building, but on closer binocular inspection it was a ship coming out of Liverpool. The Birkenhead to Belfast ferry coalesced into view beyond the wind turbines. To the west, our eyes were drawn along the Welsh coast, behind which the snow topped peaks of Snowdonia concealed the southern slopes where the Dee is born. We had reached the most northerly point of our walk; it was time for us to head south.

The tide flooded and Hilbre floated off.

1. Hilbre Point; 2. Hilbre Island, the mountains of Snowdonia in the background

4. Sealand – land where there was water

Returning to the throat of the estuary near the Flintshire Bridge, where the river cuts free from her confines, we passed my old stomping ground of Kelsterton College (now part of Coleg Cambria) in Connah's Quay.

Legend would have it that Sir Gawain forded the Dee to the Wirral in this area on his epic search for the green knight and the green chapel, a classic Arthurian tale of beheading, miraculous recovery (echoes of St. Winefride's well, where he also passed through), alluring damsels and chivalry. Nearby on Golftyn Lane stands the Sir Gawain and the Green Knight public house which has framed texts and lavish illustrations on the walls which can be perused over a fine pint of ale.

A path leading away from the main road next to Golftyn Church leads to "The Rock," which is marked on the 'Flintshire's Coast' leaflet as a viewpoint and notes that stone has been quarried from here since the time of the Domesday Book. The path to the first wooden marker doesn't immediately reveal her attractions, been blighted by litter, however, walking through the reed beds toward the Flintshire Bridge, birdsong flowed from the nearby trees and I was soon rewarded by the sightings of an egret and a primordial looking heron. As I approached the water's edge two lapwing tilted and flipped away. Lapwings are pure entertainers, on the ground they strut proudly upright and tufted like am-dram Italian generals, lustrous green shines out from their feathers giving them an alternative name of green plover, but when they take to the sky, they always give a magnificent display, twisting and drop-stalling only to recover and bank with their full, almost rectangular wings. An eco-friendly air display requiring no fuel. Not to be outdone, oystercatchers hugged the contours of the mudbanks peeping purposefully, fast, and agile. A cormorant flew low and lazy over the water carrying out reconnaissance. In the distance traffic rumbled across the sky on the bridge deck which from this angle I could see was

The Flintshire Bridge

suspended over a wharf which served as a refuge point, if needed, for mooring the Airbus A380 barge, before it reached the open estuary. The bridge is very impressive, but she has many contenders reaching to the heavens, it's as if a meeting has been called of all the pylons in the land, which are arriving from diverse directions for a synod of all their denominations at the mother power station.

I looked back inland, and the Rock and its description became self-apparent, the path I had veered away from rises upward over a stone bluff over which a row of terraced houses curve, from where they must enjoy magnificent views of the natural theatre which plays out here daily in front of the bridge. The steeple tower of St. Marks rises above all to keep an eye on proceedings. I returned toward the path grappling and re-ordering the perspective to accept the view of Dock Road from this unusual angle. The quayside was a favourite spot for us to devour our take-away chips on lunch breaks from college. I was previously unaware of a path here, a serendipitous victory, a new path always feels good, a new view gives previously familiar places fresh context. Pools of

water reflected the light, the wind on my face was cooled by the small flecks of snow remaining on the ground.

The name of Connah's Quay is a recent one, possibly deriving from an inn owner at the fledgling port. The path drops down to emerge at the back of the now sadly closed Quay House pub. In my mind a donkey jacketed stevedore stands perplexed at the closed door. A stone which was placed here to mark the high-water level of the floods of 1865 wasn't to be seen, it would have been the first of the many such markers of past floods which I would come across on my journey upstream. The hazardous shifting sands of the estuary of the wizard Dee are now complemented by the rising and falling water levels of the changeable river within a confined channel. Next to the Kathleen and May Heritage Centre I leant on the railings and was rewarded as the electric blue of a kingfisher flew above the gulley.

Following the canalisation of the Dee, a stone quay was built at the hamlet of Golftyn. By the early 19th century, it had developed into the busy port of Connah's

The view from 'The Rock' a secret gem gratefully revealed by the WCP

Quay. Coal from Northop hall, pottery, and bricks, from Buckley and steel from Brymbo were brought here for onward shipping, while pig iron, iron ore, timber, cement, and flour were offloaded here. It also became an important shipbuilding centre, the Kathleen and May, built here in 1900 is now situated in the Albert dock in Liverpool and is the last 3-masted top sail wooden schooner in Britain. On a particularly drab January afternoon, I was laid up on the couch with a bad back, Sophia was watching an episode of the 1970s drama 'The Onedin Line' on the television. The star of the show for me was undoubtedly the Kathleen and May.

An interpretation board tells that the small trammel boats fish from here for sole, flounder and plaice between July and December, while shrimp are caught from January onward. The larger boats are used for cockling. It goes on to say how the river was notoriously difficult to navigate with its shifting sands and uncertain weather, taking the lives of many fishermen. In 1889, Chester fishermen complained that Quay men had an unfair advantage as the ebb tide and narrow channel caused a salmon 'trap.' This resulted in fewer licences, increased fees, and a shorter

salmon fishing season. Pollution from the riverside factories was another problem... even 50 years ago flounders often had sores on their body. Nowadays industries are much cleaner, and fishing is good once more. Cockles and mussels are plentiful, and a greater variety of fish are caught than at any other time in living memory. If you stood here 300 years ago, the far bank of the river Dee would have been 4 miles away. Back then, a wide estuary stretched as far as the busy port at Chester which traded with ships from around the world. When the main channel began to silt up in the 1700s, the river was diverted into this ship canal.

On a balmy summer evening, juvenile sea bass flashed silver on the low tide water surface below the Kathleen and May centre from where a warden and knowledgeable volunteers led us up into the town. We followed the route of the old railway line from Buckley, seeing the scratched witness lines of the tilting locomotives in the arch of the road bridge,

as they arrived at the docks fully laden with outbound goods. With old photos in hand, we returned to the wharf side, in the exact spot where a steam crane once ran along rails to load and unload the waiting ships. A photo showed the surrounding landscape bristling with chimneys. A Connah's Quay heritage trail leaflet mentions the largest chimney in Britain in 1872 at 245ft. once stood at a chemical works at nearby Wepre Brook, Today, pylons have for the most part replaced the chimneys.

We walked along the SSSI saltmarsh, before dropping down to the water's edge to chat to a second-generation shrimp fisherman, busy taking advantage of their seasonal appearance. He told us how the recent floods had flushed them downstream to the saltwater which enables them to breed. They are sensitive to pollution, so are a good indicator of clean water. He told us he had seen no salmon this year and no flatfish for several weeks, so not all good news.

Straddling the river here are two inconspicuous structures, which on a previous solo walk I had passed without giving a second thought, their function being by no means obvious. These are the

1. An A380 wing, one of the last pair, on her way to Mostyn Dock;
2. Eventide at Connah's Quay;
3. The busy banks of Deeside

turrets for a tunnel. The Alwen reservoir was built between 1909 and 1921, to supply clean water to the town of Birkenhead to meet the demands of increasing population and industry. The water was supplied via a pipeline which crosses beneath the Dee within the tunnel at this point. The supply nowadays terminates just across the river where it feeds Tata steel and other industries, the turrets provide access for maintenance and contain fans to control moisture levels within the tunnel.

So, at this point, near where the Dee enters the estuary, waters from her headwaters some 25 miles away as the crow flies, short cut the natural meandering river flow to be carried under her sister waters, unseen and uncelebrated. The river Alwen meanwhile continues to flow into the Dee upstream of Corwen, taking the lazy route to get here. This is the first visible sign of a river with many diverse and complicated demands, the flows of which are highly regulated. More on the Dee regulation scheme later.

The Dee between Connah's Quay and Chester is flanked by a path and the number 5 cycle route, so it is possible to travel between the two points by foot and bicycle or by boat. We managed all three, on our first trip under blue skies, we decided to take advantage of the cycle route, following the signs for Chester, 8 miles distant, soon arriving at Hawarden railway bridge.

Hawarden bridge opened in 1889 when she was the largest bridge of the type in the UK, having a 285-feet opening span to allow the passage of tall ships. The two small and one larger arch of the bridge form a hop, step, and jump over the main span of the river. A masterpiece of engineering, the steam powered rams and the curved support structure are still visible as are the wheels and cogs of the turning gear. She last swung in 1960 and is now fixed in position.

The site of Shotton steelworks still dominates the landscape. The works were opened by John Summers in 1898. At its peak in the 1960s operations extended over 1,000 acres and the work force was 13,000 strong. Steel making ended in 1980 with the eye-watering loss of over 7,000 jobs, a massive blow to the local economy. The current plant is owned by Tata Steel, and now processes strip steel, the Shard in London is one of many modern buildings to use steel from Shotton. There is a fantastic history board in the Kathleen and May heritage centre made from coated steel produced on site, which gives a timeline of production at the site from 1898 to the current day.

When we went past the old red brick headquarters of the steelworks they were boarded up and forlorn, the clock face was damaged. A beautiful building in a prime riverside location, crying out to be re-purposed and cared for.

In front of her are some old jetties, the wooden deck falls and twists, heavy iron mooring bollards high on the structure look as if they are half floating in air, their wooden supports having for the most part fallen away. The ducks on the lower beams could be in for a shock when gravity and time re-locate them.

Either side of the bridge stand protective pill boxes. The long straight river section along here could potentially have been a wartime landing spot for sea planes or used as a navigation aid.

1. Sunrise from Hawarden Bridge, the former headquarters of John Summers steelworks are on the left; 2. The Blue Bridge

A short distance further on the "blue bridge" a double leaf bascule bridge opened in 1926 carries the B5441. A bascule bridge is a moveable bridge with a counterweight that balances a span, or "leaf", throughout its upward swing to provide clearance for boat traffic. By the 1960s shipping had largely ceased on the River Dee. The bridge's lifting mechanism was removed, and the roadway fixed permanently in place. No more swinging of bridges in this area.

The original Victoria Jubilee Bridge which preceded the Blue Bridge was officially opened here by William Gladstone in 1897 and consisted of 3 spans, with the centre span being retractable to allow shipping to pass through. The increasing weight of road traffic led to her replacement, the original abutments and toll cottage still exist.

This was a busy period in the taming of the reclaimed land, new gateways were opened into Wales, former marshland became fertile agricultural land and home to many new industries and their workers. It's difficult to imagine this area with no bridges at all, not much more than a century ago. The estuary had long been overseen by castles at Hawarden, Ewloe, Flint, Shotwick and Chester, and stretching back further still, to before the Romans arrived, there were Iron Age forts at Moel y Gaer on Halkyn mountain and Burton Point, but now, the mouth of the river was truly opening up. Queensferry became home to numerous industries, including specialist steel smelters, boiler makers and the suppliers of munitions during the First World War.

Nearby on the upstream side stands the more functional Queensferry by-pass road bridge carrying the A494, a solid permanent concrete structure, built in the early 1960s after the last of the tall ships had sailed past and now carrying a seemingly endless stream of traffic.

The wharves built in this area after canalisation would have been used to load and discharge all manner of commodities, such as iron, timber, and numerous foodstuffs in addition to the coal and bricks which would have been brought here by tramway.

1. Sunrise over the A494 road bridge;
2. We Three Bridges. From the Kathleen and May heritage centre wheelyboat

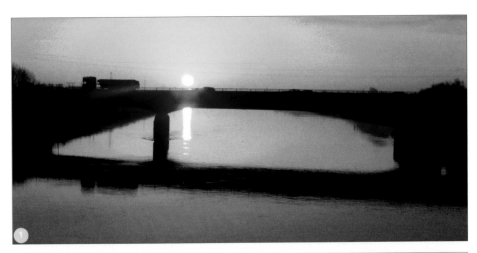

Prior to the building of the bridges, a ferry was in existence at this site. In 1743 an act of Parliament created two toll-free passages to compensate for the loss of low water fords after the canalisation of the Dee. The lower ferry located here was given the name King's ferry in 1820 when George IV became king and was re-named Queens Ferry when Queen Victoria came to the throne.

The new communities of Queensferry, Sandycroft, Saltney and Sealand were brought into existence along the water's edge, the historic riverside settlements of Moor, Rake and Manor no longer dipped their toes in the flow.

Hawarden on the hill overlooking the Dee is mentioned in the Domesday book as Haordine and is well worth a detour. It stands on the first high ground to the west of Chester, which rises from the former Saltney marsh. The old main road from Chester runs immediately below the castle which dates from the late 13th century. The castle played a significant role in the wars of independence when it was ceded to Prince Llywelyn, but later attacked by his brother Dafydd. It last saw action in the Civil War. It overlooks another 'castle', the hall which became the home of William Gladstone following his marriage to Catherine Glynne. Gladstone was four times prime minister between 1860 and 1894. He was a great reader and built up a collection of over thirty thousand books, which are now housed in 'Gladstone's Library', a memorial to his life and work. A grade 1 listed residential library, it is unique and a wonderfully atmospheric place. The west window of the church of St. Deiniol, adjacent to the library is dedicated to Gladstone and is a magnificent example of stained glass, possibly the finest in Wales.

After the bridges, the landscape opens, a flatness of fertile farmlands extends away from the northern bank. The river upstream is die straight, tamed into the Dee Navigation. New industries at Sandycroft no longer require river access, HGV's are parked up on quiet riverside access tracks, ready to return to the tarmac streams. The Dee here is restricted in its character, it's playfulness and ferocity curbed, its moods confined. I sometimes find myself trying to picture in my mind's eye an unfettered Dee, spilling out across a wide estuary, lapping at the shores of Saughall and Burton Point, though I have warm memories of this area, of going to college in Connah's Quay and work in Broughton, of sepia-toned dawns and dusks on the banks, of racing to catch the power of the bore and losing myself in the long and varied industrial and commercial history of this stretch of the river. If I had known the estuary in its wild state, where 'unbounded freedom ruled the wandering scene' I, like John Clare, who saw his beloved moors and commons trampled and imprisoned by enclosure, might view things differently.

Sandycroft. I was familiar with the place name long before I saw the village. There are few clues that I was stood at the spot which was the birthplace of the 'Royal Charter', an auxiliary steam clipper, which four years later would be wrecked on the rocks at Moelfre on Anglesey. "The Golden Wreck" by Alexander Mc Kee filled my boyhood head with tales of a gold rush on the other side of the world, and the ultimate power of nature. It was a story of adventure, riches and heroism, the final act of which was played out within a morning's walk of the house where I was raised.

Her launch here in 1855 attracted much attention due to the vast proportions of the biggest ship to be built on the Dee, and the site of its launch which was too narrow to allow a traditional 'bow first' entry into the water. In pouring rain with a large crowd watching, the 320-foot and 2,875-ton bulk of the Royal Charter became stuck fast in the mud. (Echoes of the launch of the SS Great Eastern, Brunel's behemoth all steel ship in 1858 on the Thames). It was several months later that the Royal Charter was successfully launched, on another high tide. The journey to the outfitters in Liverpool was itself not without incident, a grounding on a bend in the river near Flint castle was an inauspicious start to her travels.

She was lost on her way back from Melbourne on her sixth and final journey on the 26th October 1859, when she was driven on to the jagged rocks of the Anglesey coastline in hurricane force winds within a few hours of Liverpool. The memorial on the coast there says over 400 perished, the passenger list was not recovered, estimates of exactly how many lost their lives vary between 446 and 497. Many of those on board were weighed down with their spoils from the Australian gold rush. 'Life and Death on the Royal charter' by Chris and Lesley Holden details her story right through from her

building in the yard here, the eventful life and tragic loss, accounts of heroic lifesaving and the salvage work which has taken place on the wreck.

From 1862, the site was occupied by the Sandycroft Foundry which was established by John Taylor of the Mold mines in the Alun Valley. His foundry operated until 1926 when increasing competition forced closure. As I gazed over the river, lost in a daydream of gold and high seas, the sound, then the sight of the surge of the Dee bore brought me back to the present, an unexpected treat.

The Airbus factory at Broughton is located a short distance upstream, it was built as a shadow factory for wartime aircraft production in 1939. When construction began, the site initially appeared level but was found to have a fall of 7ft which needed extensive levelling. Trenches had to be cut to drain the existing gullies away from the factory. An account passed down from the time of construction recalls numerous eel pits in the area.

1. The Dee bore at Sandycroft;
2. The last A380 port wing slips quietly away from her loading point

From the initial production of Wellington and Lancaster bombers, the site has produced a whole range of aircraft including the ahead-of-its-time Comet, the sad in-service losses of which had the effect of bringing in many new improvements in aircraft design which are standard practice today.

My own link with the site began in 1980, when I moved from Anglesey to begin an apprenticeship at the then British Aerospace factory, though confusingly for me, many people in the area at that time still referred to the factory as 'De Havilland's' by-passing the in between incarnation of Hawker Siddeley completely. Another link with Broughton is through my wife Sophia whose father joined an RAF reconnaissance unit here during the war. He reminisced how his 'training' consisted of reading an operation manual before climbing solo into the cockpit of a spitfire. On his first flight, he clipped the top of a tree as he gained altitude. I am pleased to relate that he went on to complete many sorties over continental Europe and went on to lead a long and fulfilling life.

The piles of the 'load-out' transfer facility mark the spot where A380 wings were transferred from the road trailer to the 'Afon Dyfrdwy' river barge for the journey to the Port of Mostyn where they were further transferred to an ocean-going vessel for the ultimate destination of the final assembly line at Toulouse. The barge was designed to run aground safely on sand banks, in respect and acknowledgement of the shifting sands of the Dee. Sadly, A380 wings are no longer built and the last set were despatched in February 2020.

The Royal Charter was innovative in her day, cutting the journey time to Australia, and making it possible for greater numbers to travel, the A380 continues this process, by sky rather than sea, I wonder if the Dee will play a part in future world-shrinking developments?

At Queensferry the barge would pass under the blue bridge built by Sir William Arrol and Son, the same civil engineering contractor who built the original factory.

The footbridge at Saltney Ferry was built in 1968, it replaced the 'Higher Ferry' the second of the two toll-free passages across the canalised Dee, created by an act of Parliament to compensate for the loss of low water fords.

Interpretation boards nearby give a fascinating account of the ferry and the Manifold family, five generations of who operated the ferry here from 1760 to 1968. The ferry ran from 5.00 am to 9.00pm every day, as they had to cover all the shifts at Broughton as well as the railway sheds, nearby Mold junction being a busy 24-hour operation, as well as other industries in Saltney. The twelve-foot oars were replaced with an outboard motor in 1955 which made life easier for the ferryman and meant there was room for 15 people and their bikes.

While dawdling in the new library within the Storyhouse centre at Chester, I came across a photo of preparations being made to place two large pipes directly across the Dee in this area. A subsequent conversation with a former production manager at Welsh Water revealed that the pipeline carries water abstracted from upstream at Heronbridge. The pipeline dips under the Dee before emerging on the opposite bank where it flows onward to Prenton park water treatment works at Birkenhead. This is the second instance I have encountered in the first few miles of the Dee where waters abstracted in higher reaches are sequestered underground for downstream use, an unseen underworld of contained rivers. The water supply from Heronbridge is non-potable, requiring treatment while the supply from the Alwen is low conductivity, potable water, as it is not subject to salt run off from winter road treatment or the salinity of tidal areas.

The riverbank after Saltney Ferry bridge was lined with a very dispiriting amount of debris, mainly plastic. I have attended several big Dee clean ups in this area. On one visit, we collected 20 bags of assorted litter in less than two hours, but each fresh tide brings more. A lack of respect for our collective home.

We continued under clear blue February skies, the temperature was just a few degrees above freezing, the bright sun had deceived me into leaving my gloves in the van, a case of very cold hands curled around handlebars. At the bend in the river the English-Welsh border cuts across and continues to run down the middle of Boundary Lane in Saltney, the only urban street in England-Wales where this happens. Residents on opposite sides of the street were subject to differing lockdown regulations for the Coronavirus outbreak. The border is marked with two pillars cut from Halkyn stone, surrounded by daffodils. As we composed a photo, a couple approached the portal. "You don't want us in your photo!" he called. I responded with a request for passports as they crossed the threshold. As we chatted, he pointed to a footpath on the other side which leads from Saltney past the golf club into Chester. It is not suitable for bikes and was apparently very muddy, but it was a fruitful conversation as it didn't appear on my map.

The following weekend we walked the opposite bank to Chester, past the graffitied and door-less pillbox which stood guard at the southern end of the long straight of the Dee navigation. Chunky mooring bollards remain, from the time when this was a busy quay. We continued along the embankment on another die-straight bank, a snowy Moel Famau behind us. Our progress was slow, without the mechanical advantage of our bicycles of a week before, toward the vanishing point ahead of us. An icy wind and a sea of high tide stranded plastic bottles on the riverbank sapped our resolve. A cormorant skimmed above the water, a buzzard emerged from the leafy

The England – Wales border and start of the Wales Coastal Path

deserted golf course on our right and the delight of the brown-grey flash of a kestrel perked us up again.

Saltney derives its name from saltings, an area of coastal land which is regularly covered by the tide, it is thought that there was a civil settlement here as far back as Roman times for grazing livestock. When the railway arrived in 1846, Saltney was made of isolated cottages and farms on the salt marsh. The line to the goods wharfs initially carried coal and limestone from the Ruabon and Wrexham areas. The chain and anchor works were established soon after, and became the largest in the country, and are said to have supplied Brunel's Great Eastern.

There were many shipyards on the Dee, at Saltney, James Crichton's works produced a variety of vessels including barges for the admiralty in the First World War, and continued operation until 1935. There were also several oil works (distilling oil from cannel coal), a fertiliser plant and metal working operations. The riverside and old sidings industrial estates contain many engineering and electrical services businesses which continue to operate in Saltney.

Resuming our bicycle ride along the north bank we stopped at a badger sett, while the incoming tide surged over the muddy banks on the southern side around the base of splintered crack willow and elder.

As we entered Chester, we were at a significant point. The Dee here makes an abrupt ninety-degree, artificial change of direction, from its natural route which would have continued along the line of the cop (the raised bank which was constructed to prevent flooding) toward Blacon Point.

Why go to the expense, not to say back breaking hard work, of diverting a river? The estuary of the Dee is unusual in that comparatively little water occupies so large a basin. Much of the wide estuary is occupied by sand and flats which move with the tides and floods and dry out at low water, making navigation intricate and dangerous. It is an open estuary or funnel shaped, as compared to that of the Mersey, which is closed, and forms a pool of water which then flows between Birkenhead and Liverpool, naturally scouring out sand and sediment. The water flow of the Dee is insufficient to scour out an adequate and reliably deep navigation channel. There are several theories as to how the Dee estuary came to be so big, one is that the Mersey once had a different course, flowing through the Backford dip, to join with the Dee just downstream of Chester, forming a much larger river, another theory is for its formation by glacial action. The river did however remain navigable as far as Chester for passenger and freight traffic up to the 17th century when the accumulation of silt began to be a major problem. Man, as is our way, has probably contributed to this effect, the Earls of

Chester constructed a weir across the river to power their mills as early as the 11th century, reducing the tidal limit and the also the important scouring effect of the river.

The growth in trade brought on by the industrial revolution meant a solution had to be found to make reliable trade possible from Chester. It was decided that a new-cut, a canalised section or '*Dee Navigation*' should be made through the marshes taking the course of the Dee along the Welsh side of the coast to serve, among other interests, the increasing output of the Denbighshire coal fields. The marshes, had a reputation as being wild and dangerous, crossed by ancient paths, they were a graveyard for carriages and wagons. There are accounts of travellers meeting a violent end on the marshes, it is difficult to imagine that there was much opposition to the new cut.

Work started in 1734, over the next four years the new cut was dug through the marshes extending for five miles to Golftyn. The flow was blocked at this point by closing diversion sluices which are long since subsumed or removed, it must have been quite a sight to see the new cut filled for the first time.

The improvements to navigation were however only temporary. A depth gauge near the sluices marked the 16-feet agreed standard depth for the new navigation. This bend and another at Saltney take energy out of the natural flow of the river and are thought to have reduced its scouring effect even further, contributing to further silting, which the scheme was intended to overcome. The 16-foot standard was not achieved, limiting the size of ships able to use the river.

There were claims at the time that the Dee Navigation Company were more concerned with the lucrative new lands on the northern side of the new cut which were gradually re-claimed in Dutch polder style, than the improvements to the Dee Navigation for which they were formed. Many improvements were however made, including the building of embankments near the new estuary and the placing of groynes to divert the flow to replicate the rivers natural scouring effect. Thomas Telford was engaged from 1817, he was one of several eminent engineers who attempted to further tame the unruly Dee which eventually beat them all. Liverpool, which had far greater depths of water, developed as a more viable port.

Finchett's Gutter outfall in the fold of the bend is heavily engineered to prevent high tides or floods taking the Dee back into the memory of her ways when she would have continued in a broadly north westerly direction around Blacon point. The area to the east, known as Blacon or Chester basin would have been exposed to the prevailing westerly winds which sometimes caused vessels to be driven ashore. It is thought that the remains of shipwrecks lie beneath the feet of shoppers in the retail park which now occupies part of this area.

A Diversion Along the Old Dee Route

Old maps clearly show the flow of the Dee along a coastline on the Wirral side of the estuary. A study of modern maps prompted further deployment of boots on the ground. From Blacon Point the old shoreline leads to Saughall, which prior to my dalliance with the Dee, I'd never had the pleasure of visiting, existing in my mind only as a signpost leading off the Sealand road. A pre-visit a look at the current O.S. map showed 'Seahill Farm' straddling the contour lines in the now landlocked village. A map on the village institute wall noted that the fishermen's cottages which once stood at the Dee water's edge of this once coastal village have been demolished.

Current maps of this area are identified with several B.S/B.P. notes (boundary stones/posts) which I pictured as being large Stonehenge type uprights sitting under vast skies with the Dee estuary in the distant background. I developed the idea further, composing a mental photo of a stone marking the border which previously would have sat in a watery mid-point of the Dee but was now located high and dry in farmland. I did manage to find one, but it was small, covered in ivy and hemmed in by a hedge, not the photogenic scene I was hoping for. Charms of finches, flights of redwing and a white-bibbed red fox were my companions, no complaints, a walk is never wasted, headspace was found, the legs exercised.

We walked through handsome woodland from Saughall to Shotwick Castle which is slightly closer to Saughall than Shotwick. The castle stood on the very banks of the Dee, an artist's impression at the site shows a boat beneath the castle walls. It was built in 1093 by Hugh Lupus to protect against Welsh invasion and had a 5-storey watchtower. It was described as a fair castle in the mid-16th Century but as a ruin some 60 years later. All that remains today is a mound in a field, now well inland. It is clear to see why it was built at this location, there are extensive views over Sealand, the land where there once was sea. I was lucky enough to attend a talk entitled "Sealand – the pioneer's

The Holy Dee

paradise" given by the warden of St. Bartholomew's Church in the neo village. She began her enlightening talk by saying that 250 years ago over six square miles of this area were under the waters of the Dee.

Further up the 'coast' at Shotwick. a church was recorded in the Domesday book, today St. Michaels, is a glorious red sandstone structure. I cast my mind back to something I read many years ago that mooring rings were still visible in the walls of the church yard, I did indeed find a stone with a metal ring attached, though it could well have had an alternative purpose. After entering via the heavy 15th Century door, Sophia sought out and found the kneeling cushions made by her mum many years ago. This was the family church and I have a fond memory of emerging from an atmospheric low-lit Christmas morning service into the emerging dawn.

A leaflet inside titled the Church at the Ford describes how for many centuries this was a crossing point into Wales and later to Ireland and further afield by ship until the Dee silted up. Initially used for trading, the crossing was later used for military purposes. Henry III passed through Shotwick in 1245 and Edward I in 1278 and 1284 on their campaigns into Wales.

The ford was used continually throughout the 18th century, the last recorded crossing being in 1796 and a hazardous venture it must have been at this time by all accounts, with the sands 'shifting so much that new routes had to be followed constantly between the heaps of sand and the deep holes'. Even so, many travellers preferred the route across the estuary over the longer land route around the marshy estuary with its alternative risk from footpads.

The shoreline from Shotwick would have extended below the village of Puddington to Burton Point and onwards.

Grooves made by arrow sharpeners at Shotwick church

5. Chester – Deva – Caerlleon

When the Romans arrived in the lands of the Celtic Cornovii, they seized the opportunity to build their fortress on the sandstone ridge overlooking the river at the head of the estuary, a defendable position with a crossing point and fine harbour, they named their fortress Deva after the Dee, or Dyfrdwy, the sacred or Holy river or its goddess. In Welsh Dyfr translates as waters, Dwy as God. Two Millenia ago, the Dee already held long spiritual significance.

The modern name for Chester is said to derive from the Welsh name of Caerlleon (the fortress of the legions) which translated into the Anglo Saxon as Legacaestir. The 'legion' element was later dropped to give Ceastir which further evolved into Chester.

Many fine tomes have been written on Chester, its long and rich history. I've lived in the surrounding area off and on for four decades, but as part of researching this book I have had the joy of becoming a born-again tourist, of re-living those heady days of when I first arrived hereabouts. I will, as much as I can, for I do have a propensity to go off on tangents, confine the Chester section of this book with the city's interactions with the Dee, although as it is the story of the Holy Dee, there are some necessary digressions.

My walk through the city began with the south bank which, as far as I know, is not an estate agents' term for the area, or an indicator of any intellectual or political divide.

Deva – The south bank

A curve of crack willow and winter flattened reeds edged the track which leads up to the golf course. At the side of the seventh tee there is a plaque upon a stone which remembers Brewer's Hall Mount as the location of the largest gun used by the Parliamentary forces besieging Chester in the Civil War in October 1645. The gun which weighed approximately 8000lbs and had an eight-foot barrel was particularly used during the attack at Pemberton Parlour, which helped secure the surrender of the city in February 1646.

The city walls are remarkably close by here, it must have been a terrifying sight to see the gun being set up and used to bombard the city.

The Dee Railway Bridge is the first of the Chester bridges over the Dee. The original bridge was opened in 1846 for the Chester and Holyhead railway and was the scene of the 'Dee Bridge disaster' in the following May when the carriages of a train to Ruabon fell through into the river, resulting in five deaths. The investigation revealed the weakness of cast iron beam bridges, and brought criticism of its designer, Robert Stephenson (of Rocket fame) who came close to being accused of manslaughter. The bridge was later rebuilt using wrought iron. A painful learning experience which moved the industrial revolution forward another step. The bridge still carries the main London to Holyhead railway.

At the beginning of the nineteenth century, the Old Dee Bridge at

1. Civil War plaque at the golf course;
2. The Grosvenor Bridge

Handbridge, the only crossing point in the city, was very congested, an alternative route was urgently required to protect Chester's trade. The Grosvenor Bridge was constructed in the early 1830s, its huge 200-foot arch at that time formed the longest single span stone bridge in the world and is yet another bridge over the Dee which pushed forward the limits of engineering, it is the first stone bridge we have seen so far, and a real stunner. Constructed from red sandstone and lit at a low level from black metaled fittings in gaslight fashion, it is an atmospheric crossing point.

The bridge's great height was necessary to allow the masts of sailing ships, which were still able to travel this far upriver at that time to pass underneath. Viewed from below the large embankments on either side are prominent, the one on the city side carries Grosvenor Road/Street from Deva's sandstone ridge, not only dividing the Roodee as it does so, but also diagonally cutting through the medieval street pattern.

The bridge was built by Thomas Harrison, who as we shall soon see, had a huge impact on the cityscape of Chester.

It was opened by the thirteen-year-old Princess Victoria, five years before she became Queen. Once operating however complaints were made about excessive tolls, which were abolished in 1885, to assuage traders who were actively seeking alternative routes to carry their wares.

Harrison could not have imagined an event which was to take place over a hundred years later which would be made possible by that glorious high arch. A report in the Chester Standard from 2017 about the release of the film 'Dunkirk' celebrated the role of Flying Officer James 'Jas' Storrar from Chester who, aged just 18, had flown at Dunkirk as part of a distinguished career in the RAF. It concluded with... He was the (610) squadron's last CO when it was disbanded in 1947, but not, according to legend, until 'Jas' had flown under the Grosvenor Bridge in a Hurricane.

Adjacent to the Grosvenor bridge, running down from its supporting embankment, lies Overleigh cemetery. By 1854 many of the parish graveyards in Chester were closed and this was the only municipal burial ground in the city. Built in the 'Victorian picturesque' style, it has a lovely mix of deciduous and evergreen trees amidst an undulating landscape in which the gravestones nod and lean on each other for support. I rested on one of the curved rustic benches in the garden of reflection, which is laid out with a series of circular yew hedges to represent ripples, in recollection of the lake which once occupied the space. A quote by Thomas Hughes on the plaque at its centre sums up the cemetery perfectly 'Nature and art alike combined to produce a retreat worthy of the dead, and yet full of beauty and allurement for the living'. The grave of Mary Jonas who died in 1899 is located nearby, her inscription informs that she was the mother of 33 children which, I would say, has more than earned her spot in this wonderful resting place.

Continuing past Nowhere, the tall spire of the wonderfully identified 'Parish Church of St. Mary without-the-walls, within the Ancient Parish of St. Mary-on-the-Hill' pierced the sky. On the opposite bank, once the home to industry, herons sat high in the trees like oversized Christmas decorations. Greenway Street, the historic heart of Handbridge's salmon fishing community, leaned its cobbles to the Dee, fringing Edgars field, the metal railings of which record the association with the venerable fish.

The shrine to Minerva is on an island of red sandstone in the old Roman quarry and is the only rock cut Roman shrine still in situ in Britain. It is pleasingly accessible, but a downside is that it is lightly protected and badly eroded. Minerva wore many hats, an interpretation board advises that she was the goddess of quarrymen, wisdom, arts and crafts and (defensive) war, it goes on to say the field is named after King Edgar, the Saxon King of Wessex and all England. In 973, it is alleged that he was rowed up the River Dee by eight British princes in recognition of him being their overlord. Edgar is said to have demanded a tribute of 300 wolves' heads yearly from a prince of North Wales, which was paid for only three years, by which time wolves were exterminated out of Wales.

The Old Dee Bridge presents herself well in advance, clearly visible from up and downstream, a historic focal point at the heart of the city. She is the oldest of Chester's bridges, seven gloriously unequal arches with sandstone cutwatered piers.

There is thought to have been a fording point here since pre-Roman times which

74   *The Holy Dee*

they, no doubt, would have improved, as was their way. The early medieval bridges were probably made of timber and there are records of them having been washed away on several occasions. In 1387 Richard II granted funds for the repair of the bridge. Following his surrender, as we saw earlier, at Flint Castle in 1399, he was held prisoner in the castle which overlooks the bridge, and quite possibly would have been able to see how his money had been spent.

An interpretation board shows an artist's impression of an army crossing over the bridge on one of the medieval military campaigns into Wales. Rows of soldiers can be seen marching through the arch of the outer gateway, the portcullis having been raised and the drawbridge dropped to allow them to pass. During the civil war, supplies were brought into the city over the bridge from Wales, after the defeat of the Royalist forces at Rowton Moor, it played its part once more as Charles I escaped to Denbigh.

The outer gateway was demolished in 1782 to ease the flow of traffic, but further increases and safety concerns led to the bridge being widened on the upstream side in 1826, to provide a footway. The architect was Thomas Harrison, his improvements however were still insufficient for the bridge to cope as the single point of entry to Wales. As we have seen, Harrisons services would soon be called upon again to build the new Grosvenor Bridge.

This area today is tranquil, a relaxing intrusion as a strip of countryside runs through the heart of a busy city. The soft red sandstone sides of the river valley quarried and re-profiled since Roman times, are subsumed into the modern form of the surroundings. The great weir was thrown diagonally across an old causeway by Hugh Lupus in 1093 to divert water under the northernmost pair of arches of the bridge to power his corn mills. The building of the weir would change the dynamics of the river, raising the upstream level substantially, exacerbating flooding in times of spate, and reducing the downstream scouring effect contributing to the silting problem.

The weir is generally taken to be the tidal limit of the river, a solid barrier to the progress of the saline waters of the maritime Dee, a preventor of its mixing

1. & 2. *Edgar's Field Artwork;*
3. *The Old Dee Bridge*

with the higher fresh riverine waters. The limit of the estuary is not obvious to the casual observer as the canalised section of the river does not swell out into a visible estuary for a further five miles, where the river runs free just downstream of Connah's Quay. There are, as in many things in life, exceptions, when the movements of celestial bodies conspire in their alignments to exert the strongest gravitational pull on our little blue dot planet, the waters are heaved along with them in spring tides which can surge over the weir as far as Farndon, upsetting my convenient dividing of the river into neat categories. And rightly so, as William Blake said,

> "I wander thro' each charter'd street,
> Near where the charter'd Thames does
>   flow,
> And mark in every face I meet,
> Marks of weakness, marks of woe."

The bore, the vanguard of the flow of the biggest spring tides, is first repelled by the weir, then fills the basin with swirling muddied waters, bringing an eerie silence to the boisterous weir, before surging on over her and carrying the debris of the estuary, tree trunks, mats of reeds and hitch-hiking ducks upstream. The bore is anything but boring, we have stood here many times watching the events unfold, once overhearing a passer-by say to her friend 'doesn't the river usually flow the other way?' The quiet of the slack water of the tide is slowly broken by the return of the waters, which have washed the banks far upstream, as they ebb downstream, pulled by the turning of the earth, the orbit of the moon. As the waters return, herons take their opportunities to spear confused way-washed fish in the stirred waters. Silver tail kicking fish are held high by cormorants and shown as prizes, then quickly despatched, before they are stripped by the circling kleptoparasitic gulls. A play of the forces of nature, watched by workers on their way to lunch, in the centre of a busy city.

As long as man has existed on the banks of the Dee, he has taken advantage of its larder of salmon and other fish. After the Norman Conquest, the Earls of Chester took possession of the fishery, neither a net could be thrown or a boat launched within the boundary of the earldom without their permission, this separate jurisdiction, with its own peculiar laws was distinct from other British rivers. About 1,000 salmon were taken each year, the catches were policed by the Sergeants of the Dee. The area between the weir and the bridge is known as the King's Pool, in medieval times the fishing rights were rented out, though the Abbott of Chester and the monks could fish for free.

In 1753 forty-one salmon were landed in a single draw of the net, all of which were at least fifteen pounds in weight. Catches declined through the nineteenth century due to overfishing, leading to the establishment of Fishery Boards and the requirement for licences for the many full-time fishermen. In the early twentieth century restrictions on where fishermen could operate and the building of the fish pass allowed numbers to increase. The weir as mentioned previously has a significant effect on the river, an immovable structure built to harness the power of the river, it is a barrier to movement of fish, particularly salmon. Prior to the building of the fish pass, in times of low water levels salmon would have to wait for flows to increase or for the assistance of high tides to negotiate the weir. The turbines of the hydroelectric works at the weir would have presented a further hazard to migrating fish, while the water flows over the weir are affected by water abstractions along the length of the river to this point. The weir is a beautiful sight which affects many things, animal, vegetable and mineral. Numbers of the noble salmon sadly, continue to decline, though steps are being taken to increase their numbers by removal of obstacles and improvements to habitat, no commercial fishing is currently carried out.

Salmon are not the only interesting fish in the Dee, in 1928 a sturgeon weighing 136kg, (300lb) was caught between the Grosvenor and railway bridges. Although rarely seen in UK waters, Sturgeon are classifed as 'Royal Fish' – a status granted by King Edward II, and belong to the treasury. The fish was reported to ... the Receiver of Wrecks who act on behalf of the crown in relation to Royal Fish and to who the proceeds of the sale were due. Sturgeon, are now a protected species, it is an offence to land them, negating any Royal involvement.

At salmon leap, the concrete-toothed flats no longer recollect the hue of their name. If I were to find myself in another life and living in one of them, the views over the weir could potentially cause me to ossify into a window seat as I would watch the dawn break, the sky paint the morning, the tides ebb and flow, the cormorant's fish, the people going about their business and leisure and night fall.

In addition to the corn mills on the city side of the river, many other mills and allied industries occupied this central area of the city. 'The Miller of Dee' by Roy Wilding gives a fascinating account of the many mills, their operation over a period of centuries and the social changes which brought them into being. As the wool industry developed in the twelfth century, the first fulling mill was built to clean, shrink, and felt cloth on the Handbridge side of the Dee, an industry which would continue possibly until the eighteenth century when the mills were converted to process paper.

The leather industry would soon follow, by the seventeenth century, around twenty per cent of all craftsmen in the city were producing shoes, horse tack and many other leather articles. A mill where oak bark was ground to make the tanning liquor for use in the leaching pits was located in Handbridge, while the skinners' yards, tanneries, workshops and warehouses were mainly concentrated to the south of the city, between the walls and the Dee.

The stages in leather making were many, it is little wonder so many people were employed, though many of the tasks would have been unpleasant, such as "unhairing and fleshing". Some tanneries kept mastiff guard dogs which would 'eat flesh off hides, control vast numbers of rats, and provide excreta used in the tanning process'. By the early twentieth century, the leather industry had disappeared from Handbridge.

Handbridge had several tobacco and snuff mills dating back to the early eighteenth century, the flats at Salmon leap were built in the 1960s on the site of Nicholls tobacco and snuff mill which closed in the 1950s. The mill extended low and long toward the bridge; an old photo captioned 'the mill was busy in the 1930s' shows a line of delivery vans with flat capped drivers. Plate 10 in Picturesque Chester by Peter Boughton of an Aerial View of Chester from the East, in 1855 by John McGahey shows the buildings of the 'snuff mills' extending out into the river at

1. *The Old Dee Bridge by night; 2. Churchill House; 3. Queens Park Suspension Bridge*

right angles to the bank at the weir, the restored wheel can be seen.

I walked beneath the imposing Neo-Georgian style Capital House, built in the late 1930s as the headquarters of the Western Command of the British Army it had control over the whole of the western U.K., playing an important part in the war effort. It has been speculated that the bunkers hewn out of the sandstone beneath the building played host to secret meetings between Winston Churchill, after whom the building is now named, General Eisenhower, and General De Gaulle. Following the dissolving of the Western command in 1972, the building was eventually re-purposed as a bank, new shrines to new Gods. It is now part of the campus of Chester University.

The fourth and last of Chester's bridges, the pedestrian Queens Park Suspension Bridge, was originally built in 1852 to connect the city with the suburb of that name across the river. The current bridge was opened in 1923 and was restored in 2012. It is interesting to note that in the Aerial View of Chester from the East, a bridge is shown in position at all four locations as far back as 1855 despite

St. John the Baptist's church and the Anchorite's Cell from the Queens Park bridge

the southern bank of the Dee being far less urbanised. I hope any further bridges, yet to be built across the Dee will have as much character as the existing gang of four.

The riverside path extends beneath the bridge, past fine houses and apartments with black-metalled stairways zigzagging down the steep gardens. A kissing gate marks a swift transition from city to the open countryside of the Earl's Eye meadow. Once more we come to an 'eye' indicating that an island existed on this area of flood plain. A leaflet posted by the friends of the meadows listed the impressive wildlife seen in the preceding months, including whimbrel, common sandpipers, a tawny owl, various warblers as well as large skipper, small copper, and common blue butterflies. There is a fantastic close-up photo of a cormorant with a captured lamprey twisting around its beak, the notes mention they were in plentiful supply, I wonder if that constitutes a surfeit. This photo was much appreciated, when I had witnessed cormorants fishing at the weir, I had assumed they were catching young eels. The meadows nose toward the north bank of the Dee where sun drenched Deva terrace with its bright coloured collection of doors sits gloriously at the boat-ready water's edge. A sweep of grand designs follows; a Noah's Ark garden of animal sculptures overlooked by the queen, sumptuous glass-walled residences, black and white Tudor style boathouses. Yellow trails of willow catkins swing lazily in the breeze, I imagine long summer evenings and sundowners being taken in the gardens. The river curves deliciously south around the well-kept spaces, past sailing and motorboat clubs, the ferry crossing to Sandy Lane, sadly not running on that day. The river had a gentle busyness of rowers, canoeists, and various boards with sitting, kneeling, and standing paddlers making their way along the generous up-weir width of the lazy flow. At the end of the meadow a hedgerow was alive with birdsong, I could see fleeting movements within the hawthorn, blackthorn, and brambles as they gorged on berries and sloes before leaving in chuckling squadrons. The meadows are a wonderful area of countryside on the edge of the city.

Deva – The north bank

The peregrination continued, by returning to the Cop and following the north bank through the city.

In the 1850s thousands of tons of cheese were sent to London on boats loaded at the Cheese Stage which once stood at the Cop. Thomas Pennant, on one of his tours in the 1770s wrote "I must not omit the most valuable memorial which the Romans left to this county: the art of cheese-making, for we are expressly told that the Celts were ignorant of it till the arrival of the Romans. The Cestrians have improved so highly in this article as to excel all countries, not excepting that of Italy, the land of their ancient masters".

The smell from the sewage works tested us as we progressed upstream past cosy looking flats, from which we imagined lush riverside views and the liberal use of air fresheners.

A diversion ensued, (with justifiable links to the Dee). At Crane Wharf the waters of recent heavy rains cascaded over the closed gates at the entrance to the canal which connects to the Dee.

I followed the canal between the new riverside builds, crossing Sealand road into the Dee basin. An interpretation board informs that when the Chester Canal was built in the 1770s, it was linked to the tidal river Dee at this point so that boats and barges could reach the wharves on the river, exchange cargoes with the sea-going vessels and allow river craft to come up to the wharves on the canal. A map and a series of photos details the history of the basin, from a view of the Water Tower in 1837 showing canal boats and river craft in the foreground transferring cargoes, to the working on boats around 1916 and a 'sorry picture' of flats and barges laid up in 1935 when the basin had become a boat graveyard. Most of them were buried when the basin was filled in in the 1950s.

The board mentioned current structural problems make transfers to the Dee very difficult (on closer inspection the closed gates were of a heavy metal construction which presumably would require a crane to lift them), but finished off on a positive note with a vision to restore the river lock and also to build a new lock in the old mill race at Handbridge which could be used to access upstream areas of the Dee safely at wider states of the tide, as opposed to the current situation of the rare access over the weir on very high spring tides which can be hazardous.

Continuing up through a staircase of locks I arrived at Chester's Canal Port. Taylor's Boat Yard still stands here, though no longer trading under that name, the yard has long historical links with boat building on the Dee. The complex of canals was built to help the Port of Chester compete with Liverpool and other canals.

If history had taken a different course, the completion of a grand project would have seen another canal connecting with the Ellesmere canal at Chester, and what piece of engineering that surely would have been... but more on that later.

The course of the river curves around the racecourse, the flow only a couple of feet from the top of the bank which leads to the brown-red arch of the Grosvenor Bridge. Behind the flat green of the racecourse, the stands, the spires of Chester, the 3-stage tower of the guildhall, formerly the Holy Trinity and the Cathedral, rise in increments into the blue sky.

An exhibition at the Grosvenor Museum informed how "During the middle ages, the site was used for the annual Gottesday (Shrove Tuesday) football match, organised by the city's trade guilds. These events were very violent and 'much harm was done, some having their bodies bruised and crushed, some their armes, heads and legges,' leading to the match being banned in 1533". In 1539, Chester Mayor, Henry Gee, possibly of 'gee-gee's' fame, organised the first horse race on the Roodee. It is the oldest racecourse in the UK still in use and is also thought to be the smallest of significance at one mile and one furlong long. Located in the heart of the city, it is an unusual and popular spot for a racecourse. I can say without a shadow of a doubt that I have made bookmakers here incredibly happy over the years. Thomas Pennant would I am sure, be delighted to know that the winner of the Chester Cup in May continues to receive a Cheshire Cheese.

When I first heard the racecourse being referred to as the Roodee, many years ago, I thought it was some sort of horse-riding term, possibly an exclamation to make a horse go faster, or a victory shout to be made on crossing the winning line, but it is not so...

The legend of the Holy Rood.

In the tenth century there was a severe drought in the area. At Hawarden, Lady Trawst, wife of the governor, prayed for rain to a statue of the Virgin Mary, the image of which held a large cross called the Holy Rood which, it is said, fell upon her and killed her. The image was tried by a jury who declared that Lady Trawst had been murdered by the Holy Rood. The sentence of hanging was opposed and instead the cross was lain down on the sands of the river from where the tide carried her to some low land near the walls of Caerlleon (Chester) where she was found and buried, over which a monument of stone was erected.

The derivation of the name is therefore thought to be from 'Rood Eye' or Holy island. The account on which the legend is based however is said to come from a Saxon manuscript which may have been written to discredit the church at Hawarden. A stone pedestal, thought to have supported the cross, is very much real, and can be seen within the central area of the course. I really cannot recommend touching it for luck.

The racecourse is located on the site of the large Roman port, where superb harbour facilities were built by the experienced second legion who were a naval unit, to receive supplies from throughout the empire. Hefty stones remain, at the edges, historic props to safeguard precious glasses of race day prosecco. Known as the 'quay wall' it would have extended down to the river floor now buried deep below, the size and monumentality could also have had a defensive function for high status buildings in this area.

The Roman settlement was founded from around AD75, its location at the mouth of the estuary, in the days before the problems with silting, would have been accessible for sea going vessels which could be sailed right up to the fortress walls, allowing supplies to brought in, and trade to go out. Sitting in a curve of the snaking Dee, on the top of the sandstone ridge, the river would have afforded protection against hostile tribes to the south and west, while a defendable crossing point could be built in the Handbridge area, to allow goods and materials such as tiles from Holt and lead from Minera to be brought in.

The fortress was twenty percent larger than the other Roman fortresses in Britain, with the largest amphitheatre, capable of seating 8,000 people. It has been suggested that Deva was intended to become the capital of Roman Britain. The port could have been the base for extending the empire westwards to Ireland. The remains of a unique elliptical building have been found in the Principia or headquarters, which could support this theory.

A collection of Roman stones at the Grosvenor Museum give a great overview of life and death within Deva and its place in the wider Roman empire. The spectacular finds were predominantly made in the late nineteenth century when work was being done on the city wall which revealed fragments of Roman stonework packed into the fill of the lower courses. The stones are in a good state of preservation and are thought to have come from a cemetery outside the city walls and to have subsequently been used in the repair of the walls in the late Roman period. Why tombstones came to be used as repair material is a mystery, possibly there was a threat of attack in the latter years of the empire. Whatever the reason, the protection which the wall offered the stones from the elements gives us a fascinating insight into the beliefs in the Roman period, both in this life and the next. Pressures elsewhere in the empire led to the Romans retreating from Britain by around AD410.

Walking under the Grosvenor bridge, the presence of the castle was upon me, looking down from the high ground where it controlled the river, the port, and the route into Wales across the Old Dee bridge. An interpretation board informs that "William the Conqueror built Chester's first castle in 1070 – a timber tower atop an earth mound. During the 12th and 13th centuries the castle was rebuilt in stone and extended by successive Earls of Chester, who were some of the most powerful nobles in the country. In Norman times the castle was the seat of power of the Earl's of Chester. The first earl, Hugh lupus (Hugh 'the Wolf') held his parliament here. The last Norman earl died in 1237. Since 1301 the earldom has been held by successive Princes of Wales, heirs to the throne, in recognition of Chester's political and military importance".

In the summer of 1854, George Borrow stayed in Chester before embarking on his "Wild Wales" adventure. When thinking of the castles built by the Norman barons he would write, "I have no Norman enthusiasm, and hate and abominate the name of Norman, for I have always associated that name with the deflowering of helpless Englishwomen, the plundering of English homesteads, and the tearing out of poor Englishmen's eyes".

Soon after the castle was built, Gruffydd ap Cynan, Prince of Gwynedd was betrayed into the hands of Hugh Lupus and imprisoned here for twelve years, he is said to have been in fetters in the market place when Cynwrig the Tall, who was visiting the city, saw an

The Holy Dee

opportunity to free him and carried him away on his shoulders.

The Castle was the frontier base from which North Wales was conquered in the thirteenth century during the reign of Edward I. The exchequer, courts and prison were based here, as well as housing the garrison. Military campaigns in 1277 and 1282-1283 were launched after Llywelyn ap Gruffudd the last Prince of Wales refused to pay fealty. A further campaign was conducted in 1294-1295 following renewed Welsh revolts. The city prospered as supplies and workers from throughout England and further afield were brought through for the campaigns, and to build the ring of castles and walled towns.

The twelfth century Agricola Tower was the original entrance to the castle. On a 'secret Chester' tour we were shown into the tiny chapel of St. Mary de Castro (St. Marys in the castle) on the first floor, which was re-consecrated in the 1920s. With its altar set into the wall, stone flagged floor and vaulted ceiling, it retains its spiritual charm. Paintings on the walls

Chester Castle

are thought to date to around 1240. The metal lined door is a reminder of the days when it was used as a gunpowder store. During the civil war the castle was used as a headquarters for the Royalists (1642–6).

Between 1788 and 1813 the outer bailey was completely rebuilt in the neoclassical style by Thomas Harrison. The buildings still serve as the courts, and regimental museum, but the military finally withdrew in 1999. The outer bailey area would historically have been used by Farriers and Fletchers (arrow makers) and blacksmiths.

The names of the various tradesmen in this area takes me back to an evening when we saw the "Mystery Plays" performed at the Cathedral. Within the program was a leaflet which listed the various guilds in Chester in the sixteenth century and the plays they were responsible for performing. The guilds were Butchers, Capper Pinners, Weirdrawers, Fletchers, Bowyers, Coopers and Stringers, Cordwainers, Hewsters, Innholders, line Drapers and Bricklayers, Masons, Mercers and Spicers, Ironmongers and Ropers, Merchant Drapers, Painters, Saddlers and Curriers, Smiths, Furbers and Pewterers, Tanners, Weavers, Wrights and Slaters.

Pertinent to the area we are in are the Water Drawers of the Dee and the Wet and Dry Glovers, who were responsible for "Noah and the ship" and "The rising of Lazarus from death to life" respectively.

The origin of the plays lies in the feast of Corpus Christi when they were performed by the monks in the Benedictine Monastery. The tradition survived until 1575 when the last performance was made, the texts miraculously survived and in the 1950s the plays were reborn after an interval of nearly 400 years and are now performed every five years. It is a true community effort, the cast is huge, we saw the opening nights performance, which was very slick, clearly the result of much preparation. The logistics alone of having some 250 performers with another 150 or so people behind the scenes was something to behold.

The history of the Benedictine monastery is one part of the huge role of religion at Chester since the earliest of times to the present day, on the banks of the Holy river. There had been a church on the site of the monastery since the seventh century, it is possible this was preceded by an even earlier Roman site of worship. The church was rededicated to St. Werburgh in 875 after the saint's relics were moved there from Hanbury in Staffordshire to protect them from an invading Danish army.

St. Werburgh was a Mercian princess with whom miraculous tales are associated, one involves wild geese who were damaging crops. Werburgh instructed that the geese be locked away in a church overnight. In the morning she told them to leave the crops alone and let them fly free. Rather than fly off, however, they circled the church honking in distress, she then noticed one of the geese was missing. Discovering that the missing goose had been eaten, she requested the carcass, which was miraculously restored to life, and peace to the fields.

In 1092 the Saxon church was transformed into a large and well-endowed Benedictine abbey. A Benedictine nunnery was also established around 1150, to the north of the castle.

The thirteenth century saw the arrival of the friars in Chester, the first to arrive were the Dominicans or Black Friars who occupied a precinct to the south of Watergate Street, they were soon followed to their north by the Franciscans or Grey

Friars. The last to arrive were the Carmelites or White friars who set up their home to the west of Bridge street. At the end of the fifteenth century, the friaries were flourishing, and rebuilding was being carried out.

The reformation would bring in major changes to the religious communities in Chester. The Benedictine monastery was dissolved in 1539. Henry VIII created a new diocese of Chester, the diocese needed a cathedral for its bishop, the old monastery church was reconstituted as 'the Cathedral Church of Christ and the Blessed Virgin Mary in Chester'. The building escaped the fate of other monasteries in the country, as we witnessed at Basingwerk and will see again at Valle Crucis. The cathedral would not be reduced to romantic ruins, artists and writers can console themselves, if need be, with inspiration from the grand structure which is very much standing and continues to serve locals, and to welcome tourists.

J. S. Howson quotes an earlier antiquarian to show what picturesque effects have been lost by the destruction of the friaries. "In 1597 the white-freeres steeple curiously wrought, was taken downe, and a faire house built there by Sir Thomas Egerton, knight lord keeper: a great pitie that the steeple was put away, being a great ornament to the citie. This curious spire steeple might still have stood for grace to the citie, had not private benefit, the devourer of antiquitie, pulled it down with the church, and erected a house for more commodity, which since hath been of little use. So that the citie lost so goodly an ornament, that tymes hereafter may more talk of it, being the only sea-mark for direction over the bar of Chester". He goes on to say how there was a time when Bridge Street must have been 'singularly curious and pleasing in the light and shade, in the projections and corners, of its church-architecture: for old St. Bridget's stood there, close under the Carmelite Spire, and opposite St. Michael's and St. Olave's, with one of which churches it was united by an arch over the street. St. Peter's at one extremity of the street, still exhibits architecture which is anterior to the reformation'.

The sites and lands of the other two friaries and the nunnery also fell into lay ownership, the chancel arch from the nunnery is now located in Grosvenor Park. The names of the institutions which once constituted a major portion of the land within the walls and played such a part in daily life are visible in the names of the byways, Nun's Road, Black Friars Street, Grey Friars Street, White Friars Street. The Franciscans returned to Chester in 1875 with a Friary between Grosvenor and Cuppin Streets, while the Benedictines have a presence in the suburbs at Curzon Park Abbey, where they moved to in 1988 from Talacre Abbey.

Continuing the walk from the castle, the area near which became known as the Gloverstone, due to the leather workers in this area, while Skinners Lane ran between the city walls and the river. As the name suggests, this was the home of the workshops of animal skinners and tanners as well as an acid factory, and small mills. Plate 112 in Picturesque Chester, 'Skinners Yard' by Francis Nicholson shows the yard leading down to the water's edge where a boat lies waiting for trade. In the background thick black smoke rolls out of a line of chimneys partly obscuring the castle.

Skinning, leather working and the other pungent industries in this area would have made the air in the city, carried by our prevailing south westerly winds, I would think a little ripe, which may have contributed to the county purchasing and demolishing the buildings in the early 1830s. 'The Miller of Dee' recounts leather workers moving from the south side of the city to the old Handbridge Quarry site, near to the bark mill at that time.

The area now taken by the University of Chester (The County Hall building) once contained the County Gaol, which was also built by Thomas Harrison, in 1807. The Shipgate, which gave access to the quays here was taken down around 1828, no longer required. Shipgate Street still runs to the bottom of the hill upon which the medieval church of St. Mary-on-the-Hill was built by the Normans to serve Chester castle, its original foundations remain. The present church dating from the 14th century was damaged during the civil war and rebuilt. To provide a clear line of fire during the Jacobite rebellion of 1745, the upper stage of the tower was demolished, thirty feet would be added back on in the restoration of 1861-62. The church was decommissioned in 1972, I peered through the gates which were sadly locked, the building is now used as a creative space, an evening of Spanish guitar was advertised. I am sure it would have been a tranquil evening in a building which has endured and survived many throes of history.

The Bridgegate, another point which has witnessed much history over the last 2,000 years. The weir guides the waters to the Dee mills which would have stood adjacent to it. When built these were the manorial mills which would have been a very lucrative enterprise, corn grown in the area at that time would have to be brought to the mill, the miller would take his cut, usually a sixteenth, but corn varies in quality and calculating the cut was often a cause of conflict. The folk song 'The Miller of the Dee,' shows the miller living a happy independent and unattached life,

> *There was a jolly miller once,*
> *Lived on the River Dee,*
> *He danced and sang from morn till night,*
> *No lark so blithe as he.*
> *And this the burden of his song,*
> *For ever used to be:*
> *I care for nobody, no, not I,*
> *If nobody cares for me.*

I have seen several versions of the song, while the first verse remains constant, subsequent verses are sometimes more conciliatory to the miller, for example:

> *A coin or two I've in my purse,*
> *To help a needy friend.*

> *A little I can give the poor,*
> *And still have some to spend.*

The wheels of the mills turned here for a long time, undoubtedly many millers used their monopoly for their own greed, in 1237 there was a riot in which the mills were torn down, but I would like to think that some acted in the manner of the above words. They did not always enjoy a bonanza, in the mid-fourteenth century, when the Black death swept through the city the rents were reduced by up to a third, but they still struggled to make a profit. They suffered damage many times due to floods and were burnt down on several occasions.

Old photos show the mills, tall, dark, Blakeian. They were exceptionally large compared to 'typical' rural flour mills, at one time sharing the accommodation with a paper mill, however time and tide wait for no man, the incoming tide would back-up the tail race and stop the water wheels, forcing the millers to work to the rhythm of the sea. The mills burnt down for the last time in 1895 and were finally demolished in 1910, bringing some eight centuries of milling to a close. The site was taken by the hydroelectric power station which operated from 1913 until the 1940s. Proposals have been made for the return of the generation of hydro power, clean and green, from the Holy waters.

In 1601 John Tyrer constructed an octagonal tower on one of the towers of the Bridgegate to raise water from the Dee and pipe it to the city. From the modern gate, the delights of Chester are in touching distance, the Bear and Billet pub almost literally so, I was somewhat disappointed to read that the name is thought to derive from the heraldic device of the Earl of Shrewsbury who she was built for, which shows a bear tethered to a post (billet.) When I first frequented her creaking and welcoming interior some four decades ago, I was told she was named after the practise of Russian merchants billeting here, while a bear was left on board to guard the stock.

The medieval Bridgegate guarded the only approach from Wales and was therefore known as the Welshgate. Before proceeding further on my travels into Chester, I thought it would be pertinent to do some checks. "It is legal to shoot a Welshman with a longbow inside the city walls of Chester after midnight" is often quoted. I checked with the archive offices at Chester who advised me that they receive this enquiry from time to time and kindly provided me with a copy of their notes, which I have extracted from in italics as below:

At the beginning of the fifteenth century Cheshire and the Welsh borders were in a ferment. In the year following Henry IV's seizure of the throne in 1399, the Welsh rose in a rebellion which continued for several years. The situation was made much worse in the summer of 1403 when Henry Percy, hitherto a loyal servant of the new king joined the revolt and reached Chester.

Henry issued an order to reduce the risk from dissident Welshmen in the city. Its provisions included expulsion of all Welsh people – or people of Welsh extraction or sympathies – from within the walls and a ban on their entry before sunrise or their staying after sunset "under pain of decapitation," a ban on the carrying of arms by any Welshman, "apart from a knife to cut his dinner," no

Welsh person was to enter a tavern, and any gathering of three or more Welshmen was illegal.

Good news in that I am safe from arrows, but if I tarry, I may lose my head? The notes go on:

It is probably not the sort of edict which was formally repealed; more likely it was simply left to fall into disuse. The order was issued as part of the Palatinate jurisdiction of the earldom of Chester, the last vestiges of which were abolished in 1830. So, for at least the last 175 years, Welsh people have been able to sleep easy within the city.

A link to an informal document produced by the Law Commission's Statute Law Repeals team answering some of the queries that they regularly receive about various alleged old laws, gives a similar answer but finishes with the less prosaic, but equally reassuring statement:

Unlawful killings are today covered by the criminal law; see also Art. 2 of the European Convention on Human Rights on the right to life.

Above the streets of Chester

So, I get to keep my head as well, which is always a bonus. The Welsh rebellion was of course the war of independence led by Owain Glyndŵr. If Glyndŵr and the English allies working against Henry IV had been successful, and the 'Tripartite Indenture' (see later) had come into effect, he would have had control of a substantial part of the west of England, not only could I keep my head, but I could also nip into a café for a panad with a slice of bara brith.

When I do venture into the city, as I often do, in the complete safety of modern times, I sometimes take my copy of 'A Picturesque Chester' by Pete Boughton with me along the Via Principalis and other streets, gazing up at features and inscriptions and wondering what treasures lie below my feet. I sometimes refresh at an underground table next to a

The Holy Dee

Roman hypocaust in a café on Bridge Street or continue my reverie in a moment of quiet contemplation at St. Peters at the heart of the old Roman settlement or go further again to the contained vastness of the Cathedral, a huge weight of red sandstone around which the city spins and the walls slow. But these delights are well covered elsewhere, I must keep my wanderings to the fringes of the Dee.

From the Bridgegate I resume my walk along my favourite stretch of the walls which always takes me the longest time to walk, not that that is any detriment, in fact it complements the walk, I have spent many happy hours here watching the river slide past, the birds going about their business, overstaying my allotted car parking period as I wait for the sight of just one more leaping salmon, nobly connecting the salt water and the fresh.

Onwards, past the recorder steps where local artists display their work along the base of the city wall into the Groves, Chester's riverside promenade which dates to 1725. A place of ice creams and refreshments, an Edwardian bandstand, plenty of benches to while away an hour. Pleasure boats depart from here for cruises up the Dee, motorboats provided the gentle background hum to a summer's day.

I took a diversion, a short distance away from the river, up along a cobbled lane to a building which has played a long and important part in the history of Chester. At its entrance I found once more myself battling the temptation to be drawn off course, this time to the adjacent site of the Roman amphitheatre, discovered in 1929 during building work at the Ursuline Convent School. It was almost

1. *The tide silences the weir;* 2. *The return of the tide;* 3. *Feeding Stations*

immediately lost again to a proposed new bypass road. Thankfully, an appeal resulted in the route of the new road being deflected around the site. The southern half of the site remains covered and unexcavated, waiting for its history to be revealed.

The Parish church of St. John the Baptist is the former Cathedral and later the Collegiate Church of Chester. There are fantastic interpretation boards all around the church which give an excellent history of this amazing edifice, which has played its part in so many of Chester key events of which I can only give a brief overview here. The ancient church was founded in AD 689 by Aethelred King of Mercia. As mentioned earlier, it was here that King Edgar was rowed in 973 to receive homage from the sub-kings of England, Scotland, and Wales. St. John's was the city's first Cathedral, in AD 1075, Bishop Peter of Lichfield moved the seat of his diocese to Chester and began to build a cathedral church. In 1102, the see was moved to Coventry, but St. John's remained an important collegiate church. (A collegiate church being one without a bishop's see, or place where a cathedral church stands).

J. S. Howson covers the history of St. John's in wonderful language 'Chester is not only a cathedral city, but a city which possesses two cathedrals...the number of vassal-kings is not quite certain. It rises in fact, in the narratives of successive chroniclers from six to eight... As the waters of the river Dee are rich in recollections of the close of the Saxon period and the beginning of the Norman, so also are the city-walls of Chester, around which the river sweeps in bold broad curves on its way to the sea...we find in St. John's, a permanent and very grand memorial of the early Norman Period... Chester, however, still retains on the very edge of its historic river, a striking monument of its early diocesan dignity. The gigantic round Norman piers of the nave stand just as they stood in the days of William Rufus'.

Following the Reformation in the 16th Century it became a Parish Church. In 1582, unable to maintain such a large building, which would have been more than twice the length of the church today, the parishioners built a new east wall, the east end was cut off from the main body of the church and now survives as ruins outside the building.

So, Chester does indeed have its romantic ruins, which have inspired many artists, including Turner who sketched the church in city views across the Dee. A particularly interesting feature high up within one of the walls, is a small 13th century coffin bearing the inscription "Dust to Dust". Found by the Sexton in the 19th Century and set into the wall on the Vicar's orders. I clearly remember the first time it was pointed out to us... by torchlight on an atmospheric ghost tour.

Parliamentary soldiers placed a battery of cannon in the churchyard when Chester was besieged during the Civil War. Great damage was done to the city, when it surrendered in 1646, all the houses around St. John's were in ruins and the church was reduced to a battered wreck.

'The River Dee' goes on to mention the 'lofty tower, erect though mouldering, rivalling in elevation the tower of the present Cathedral, which stands on the highest ground in the city'. The book was published in 1892, after the collapse of the great tower, though the preface is dated 1875 when it would have been still standing. St. John's was heavily restored in the nineteenth century, the original medieval porch had to be rebuilt after the collapse in 1881, the sound was heard for miles around, the historic skyline changed.

The churchyard overlooking the Dee is a fine spot to watch to watch the goings-on on the river. An interpretation board here titled the 'Church on the cliff' mentions that King Edgar was rowed to St. John's by eleven British and Norse princes. The Anchorite's Cell sits on an island of rock within the former quarry from which the stone to build St. John's came, it does not get much more local than that. An ancient legend claims that King Harold did not die at the Battle of Hastings but fled to Chester where he lived the holy life of a hermit in the Anchorite's Cell. An atmospheric spot to get away from it all. The current building was restored in Victorian times and dates from the 14th century but may well have replaced an earlier structure.

Back down the cobbled path under another old quarry face, in a quiet corner of Grosvenor Park, I found, after a few fruitless but highly enjoyable circuits of the park, the re-erected St. Mary's Nunnery Arch which had been removed around 1840 and relocated to the park... This may have been relocated from St. John's Churchyard in 1871.

This is not the only arch to reside in this area of the park, which was previously unbeknownst to me, two further arches are unexpectedly stood nearby.

The Old Shipgate Arch once spanned the medieval Shipgate in the city walls, just to the west of the present Bridgegate as mentioned earlier. An interpretation board goes on to say that outside the walls there were once quays for seagoing vessels and at one time a ferry. It was moved from the city wall around 1828 to abbey square, placed in the Groves in August 1897 and on to its present location in the park in 1923 (a well-travelled arch).

Not to be outdone, St. Michaels Arch is also in the garden, relocated from St. Michaels Church which is otherwise still standing on the junction of Bridge Street and Pepper Street. This arch may also have arrived from St. John's Churchyard.

It is an unlikely though picturesque setting, arches originally made as bold statements to convey people to sites of worship or commerce, now chaperone young lovers, and conduct squirrels, and dog-walkers through this quiet area of the park. A retirement home for arches, but better they are relocated here to tell their stories than reduced to rubble. I wonder if they will still be in this spot 100 years from now.

Back at the riverside, I checked the passing flotilla of pleasure boats for any hidden kings being rowed by princes, so that I may quantify them, and resolve the number conundrum in my mind, but seeing no sign of any homage being offered, I continued under the Queens Park Suspension Bridge.

I walked along the front through memories of long-necked swans, tea rooms and Sunday afternoons, a jazz band at the Boat House, a friends-of-Keith inveiglement into the rowing club, past the kebab-stop car park from a previous life, and up Dee Lane and on to Boughton where a leper hospital stood, well outside of the city walls.

The stone tablet of St Giles Cemetery standing on the brow of the hill encapsulates the incredible history of this spot. The last two lines are a little faded and worth spelling out "When the Protestant martyr George Marsh was burnt at the stake on Gallows Hill close by

1. The arch from St. Mary's Nunnery viewed through the Shipgate; 2. St. Giles Cemetery

ST GILES CEMETERY

HERE STOOD THE LEPER HOSPITAL AND CHAPEL OF ST GILES FOUNDED EARLY IN THE
12TH CENTURY AND ENDOWED BY SUCCESSIVE NORMAN EARLS OF CHESTER THEY REMAINED
IN CONSTANT USE UNTIL 1643 WHEN DEFENSIVE MEASURES DURING THE SEIGE OF
CHESTER NECESSITATED THE DEMOLITION OF BUILDINGS OUTSIDE THE CITY WALLS. THE
CEMETERY REMAINED TO MARK THE SITE AND IN TIME THE LITTLE VILLAGE OF SPITAL
CLUSTERED ROUND IT. IN 1644 THE ROYALIST DEFENDERS SUFFERED GREAT LOSS OF LIFE IN
A GALLANT SORTIE IN BOUGHTON AND MANY OF THE FALLEN WERE BURIED HERE IT WAS ALSO
USED FOR VICTIMS OF THE PLAGUES WHICH RAVAGED THE CITY IN THE 16TH AND 17TH CENTURIES
BEING EXTRA PAROCHIAL THE SITE WAS GRANTED TO THE CORPORATION BY CHARLES II IN 1685 AS A
BURIAL GROUND AND THOUGH FOR A PERIOD IN THE CHARGE OF ST JOHNS PARISH IT REMAINS IN THEIR HANDS
WHEN THE PROTESTANT MARTYR GEORGE MARSH WAS BURNT AT THE STAKE ON GALLOWS HILL CLOSE BY
HIS ASHES WERE COLLECTED BY HIS FRIENDS AND BURIED HERE. THE LAST BURIAL TOOK PLACE IN 1854

A summertime view from the meadows

his ashes were collected by his friends and buried here. The last burial took place in 1854." An obelisk stands nearby to the memory of his death in the 1550s, an account of the execution says, 'a barrel of tar was set above his head to drip on him as he burned'.

On a more sanitary note, Boughton, sitting on the high ground which deflects the course of the Dee to the south west around the delicious sweep of the Earl's Eye, has long played a key part in supplying water to the city. The Romans were known to have used water flowing from a well in the area, which was piped to the fortress, the wellhead was marked by an altar. Boughton Water Works now extracts water from the Dee to supply the city. A walk down the hill, along sandy lane brings me to the Sailing and Canoeing club, a great spot to take advantage of the waters in a bit of healthy fun.

It is time to leave Chester, the largest settlement on the Dee, I reflect on the impact of the city on the Holy river, with its two cathedrals, three friaries, a monastery, nunneries, numerous churches, a religious martyr. There are many, many churches, and places of worship which I have not covered and indeed those which I have, could have been described in much more depth, but time is fleeting and the river rolls on. I have only scratched the surface of the history of the city. What it would be like to have x-ray eyes to see under the surfaces of the streets and buildings, what a story the stones could tell.

The (mostly) sea water shielding weir is now behind me, a new phase of the Dee begins, the plains of the borderlands. The anadromous salmon can continue with me, as stealthy, adaptable companions. With eager anticipation for the journey ahead, I follow in the footsteps of J. S. Howson, who wrote "whether it is from some reminiscence of the Druids, or from whatever cause, the 'holiness' of this 'wizard stream' meets us at every turn: so that a sacred mystery seems to brood over its waters."

THE LOWLAND DEE

6. Borderlands, Lost Holy Houses

As we joined 'The Marches Way footpath' three ducks flying in close formation reminded me of Hilda Ogden's front room. We walked against the surging flow, past arthritic crack willows, taking layers off and putting them back on again as sun alternated with shade in a chilling wind. The water level was a few feet off the top of the bank, the flood plain stood ready. Deep mud on the path caused dog walkers to retreat, the red sandstone walls of a quarry site were topped with ash trees which sent down knotted roots in search of water and nutrients. A blackcap sat low on a Branch as we arrived at Heronbridge where a few houses came closer to the river for a look. A Roman farming outpost existed in this locality, over which a battle cemetery has been found. Skeletons with savage sword cuts have been dated to the early seventh century and are thought to be from the 616AD battle between Aethelfrith of Northumbria and the Britons which we shall learn more of later.

Alder trees lined the bank like delicate paints dabbed on canvas. I waded through deep mud to satisfy my curiosity for a plaque on a fairy doored oak tree which commemorates three war veteran brothers. Two cormorants, the fishiest of birds, sat on a low Branch awaiting a meal to be carried downstream. The sight of vivid blue on the opposite bank caused us to reach for our binoculars, only to be disappointed by some plastic waste.

The tower of St. Mary's Church, which dates from the late 19th century rose above the tree line. There has been a place of worship in the village of Eccleston since the twelfth century, 'Eccles' derives from an ancient word meaning church while tun is Old English for enclosure or settlement. The churchyard contains the family graves of the Westminster family of the Eaton

Estate on which the village sits.

I imagined the tranquillity of the valley here before the A55 was built as we walked beneath the sleek grey concrete bridge. Shuttering lines are still visible from the forming of the roadway sections, metallic expansion plates clanked as heavy traffic hurried above our heads, not a place to dwell.

Nearing the village, dark clouds enveloped us, the light faded. Primroses on the opposite bank gave some yellow cheer. We saw another cormorant, this time on top of a tree stump, silhouetted against the grey sky. He dropped to the water, floating down a short distance before diving, into the silty gloom to look and probe for his tea. Long tailed tits played in the trees as we arrived at Eccleston Ferry. I kayaked from here to Chester some years back with our son Siôn, a halcyon day on the river, fresh air, and kingfishers.

A painting in the Grosvenor museum 'Ecclestone Ferry, 1853 by Henry Clowes Senior' shows a man on horseback, presumably a local farmer, escorting a short horn cow and calf using the hand operated ferry to cross the Dee here. An accompanying description informs that

The autumn riverbank

the ferry is mentioned in the Domesday book (1086) and continued in use until the mid-1940s.

I left Eccleston Ferry on a morning so grey that I feared if I stopped for too long, I might dissolve into the light mist. The path took me through tall trees and truncated sandstone spurs. Hellos! were exchanged with technicoloured kayakers slicing through the gloom. A black and white open sided building on top of a tall sandstone tower looked like a lost corner of Deva which had floated off on the affluent Dee on a particularly high tide. An open grass slope led up to a grey stone arched, balustraded viewpoint at the bottom of the Eaton estate, behind which sat an estate house, of red brick and black and white triangulated wood, topped off by blue-crested twisting chimneys. I looked back at the entrance gate, on the pillar of which was the Grosvenor family coat of arms, a gold wheatsheaf (garb) on a blue (azure) background which the family adopted in the late 14th century following a dispute over their previous coat of arms which featured a diagonal gold band or 'bend or'. All had been well with their choice of arms until Sir Robert Grosvenor and Sir Richard Scrope had both turned up in support of Richard II in a campaign against the Scots, with identical coats of arms. The subsequent dispute over which family had the right to use the arms took several years to resolve. Courts of chivalry were held at numerous locations across the land where a vast number of witnesses of varied ranks and ages including a prince, a duke, three earls, three barons, three abbots, two priors and nearly one hundred and fifty knights, esquires, gentlemen, and others were examined for one or other of the contending parties, to testify who had used the arms and when. Amongst the witnesses were Geoffrey Chaucer and... one Owain Glyndŵr, who testified in favour of Sir Robert Grosvenor. The ruling however went against the Grosvenor family who then adopted the ancient arms of the Earl's of Chester. The dispute was not quickly forgotten, nearly five hundred years later, a horse belonging to Hugh Lupus Grosvenor, the first Duke of Westminster, won the Derby. It was called Bend or.

The main hall was too far away to see, it has been rebuilt several times; the early 1970s modernist house was altered to the present French chateau style in the early

1990s. I heard the bells of the estate church and then spied her spire through the trees. Pennant mentioned that at the conquest in 1066 there was a fishery at Eaton which employed 6 men and yielded 1,000 Salmon, during its existence, the minister at Eccleston claimed the twentieth fish.

The path short-cutted the 'Crook of Dee' a horse-shoe shaped bend in the river, I was cheered when the path re-joined the river, and the contents of my wallet were undiminished. An estate house had a plaque marking the flood level of 9th February 1946, it was about 18" up the wall, above a couple of steps, the house sat well above the river level, which was a fair distance away, that must have been quite a flood.

A drainage channel arched by a delicious stone bridge led down from the estate to a weir which had a ramp, hopefully as an aid for otters to access a long thin lake shown on the map as 'the serpentine'. I smelt wild garlic for the first time in the season as a blackcap flitted in red dogwood, which was mud stained by a receding water level.

Aldford brook drained a large area of West Cheshire into the Dee through a haze of wispy spring willow buds on the opposite bank. Up ahead I could see the graceful blue and white arch of Aldford Iron Bridge curving over the river between sandstone abutments. This is far more than a functional bridge and well worth a lengthy pause to admire its pure class, which receives little use. Designed by Thomas Telford and built in 1824 by William Hazeldine, these two gentlemen have gifted us further delights upstream.

Sophia joined me, the bridge taking us in some style to the opposite bank, where we followed a footpath up the hill toward the church of John the Baptist in the village of Aldford. As we approached, we could see a mound to the right of the church, its outer wall dropping off into a ditch or moat, before rising again to the centre of what is undoubtedly a motte and bailey. A notice in the porch of the church advises that it is a historic English Heritage scheduled monument and the best surviving medieval motte and bailey in Cheshire, therefore the dumping of soil, grass clippings etc. is an offence under the archaeological areas act 1979. Adjacent to the bailey a fantastic old hollow oak tree stands which, I am sure, has witnessed its share of historical events as well as

Aldford bridge

gardening transgressions at this site.

There has been a settlement in Aldford, the old ford, since at least the 11th century, the motte and bailey were likely to have been built to protect the river crossing into Wales and the city of Chester. St. John's was built in the nineteenth century, along with most of the rest of the model Eaton estate village. An ancient cross in the graveyard is identified with a plaque dated 1901, which honours memory of Hugh Lupus Duke of Westminster, whose family still own the estate. The old wooden stocks built into the wall alongside the main Chester road date back to the seventeenth century.

As we left Aldford and the Marches Way, a power boat went downriver breaking the natural symphony. The Marches Way continues south broadly following the route of the Dee before seeking out Malpas on its 218-mile journey linking Cardiff with Chester. At a beautiful, wooded curve three mandarin ducks took off from a drainage channel, a chiffchaff called, a woodpecker drummed above our heads, we walked over a white blossom confetti path, simply perfect. The river took a broad semi-circular sweep around waterlogged fields before we passed the

Aldford stocks

last half timbered, swirled-brick chimneys of the Eaton estate.

Next to the township of Poulton, my map shows the footprint of an airfield where RAF Poulton was operational from 1943 until 1945. Going further back in time, Poulton Abbey was founded in this area by the Cistercians around 1153, but the abbey was short lived, relocating in 1214 to a site near Leek in Staffordshire where it became Dieulacres Abbey. By the 16th century the abbey buildings had been lost, these are

not the only holy houses to have been lost near the Dee, as we shall see further upstream. Recent excavations here have revealed the foundations of a medieval chapel and associated graveyard. Roman and earlier finds have also been made in this archaeological treasure trove.

We followed a curved westerly dovetail of the river to its southern edge where the map showed the black crossed line of the border between England and Wales extending from Pulford village re-joining and accompanying the mid-point upstream. We were facing back toward the tower of Aldford church which we had passed an hour before "that's not fair!" said Sophia at our seeming lack of progress, on this voluptuous stretch of the river. Emerging into open farmland, from an overgrown path, we glanced back at a sign which stated, 'diverted by legal order'. We hurried on, mindful that ignorance is no defence in a court of law just in case there was a stealthy official, waiting to leap out of a bush and issue a retrospective summons upon us. Pulford Brook joins the Dee from the west, a silver line of water running under an old stone bridge, which sat pleasingly in front of Hope mountain. The power boaters returned, kayakers rode their bow waves, chaffinches bounced on the boughs of wispy spring goat willow.

We walked past noble stands of old oaks, the river made a fiddlehead turn almost heading back whence it came through holiday chalets some on stilts, some still wearing their winter coats while others had mowed lawns leading down to the bank. Rickety scaffold pole landing stages were emerging from winter floods, mud-spattered debris-trailed to a boat sitting marooned on a bank of muddy goo, its transom full of silt, its nose pointing up at the moon, like a badly placed welcome to a seaside town awaiting bedding plants to replace the mud and flotsam. This area is shown on the map as Almere, I have heard it referred to as Almere Ferry, roads heading toward a common point on the river would seem to support that a ferry did operate here in the past. The Alun joins the Dee with no fanfare amid the holiday chalets, her twenty-five-mile twisting flowing tale from Cyrn-y-Brain now joining the story of the Dee. We heard the hum of pumps at a fish farm just as we were hit hard and fast by an April shower which had crept up un-noticed behind us, bringing the recent warm and dry spell to a sharp and soggy end.

Arriving at Farndon, we said goodbye to the uppermost tidal limit of the Dee, which by my reckoning, makes the very last section of the Alun, on an ultimate spring tide, for the briefest of times and the shortest of stretches, a tidal river. We were now, for sure, leaving the maritime section of the Dee behind us and were truly in a freshwater river plain. Vertical red sandstone cliffs mark the entrance to Farndon, from a distance, a perfectly formed oak poised on the cliff edge looked like a bonsai tree arrangement, it was extremely easy on the eye. Big comfortable looking houses sat square above the oblique lines of the cliffs, an interpretation board nearby identified this feature as cross bedding within the Dee cliffs at Farndon which are a site of special scientific interest (SSSI), dating from the Triassic Age (250 – 200 million years ago).

At the top of the sandstone ridge, the curving churchyard of St. Chads sits in a quiet location at the heart of the village. A large ancient yew near the porch may have been witness to the musket shot holes being made in the walls during the civil war in 1643 when soldiers were billeted inside and fighting reached the churchyard. The Parliamentarians fought their way over the bridge into Wales, a Royalist stronghold, the church was severely damaged in the fighting, and by 1645 it was derelict. Today it is altogether a more peaceful spot, the beautifully restored Civil War Window of 1662 is a reminder, particularly of the instruments of war used in those turbulent times.

We crossed the venerable old bridge from England into Wales, from Farndon to Holt, from Cheshire to Wrexham, we were neither chased by roundheads nor stopped by Royalists, nor charged a toll to pass, as was the case for more than 500 years. Others may not have been so lucky. On dark nights according to legend, it is said the screams of two murdered boys can be heard here. In 1282 John de Warenne, 6th Earl of Surrey was rewarded for his support of Edward I in his subjugation of the Welsh princes with lands which included Dinas Brân castle at Llangollen. The two boys of the castle were made his wards, but de Warenne, eager to acquire their lands, cast the sleeping boys off the bridge in a late-night return across the bridge from Chester on his way to Holt castle.

The middle arches were clogged up with bleached tree trunks and debris both organic and not so organic. The lower parts had been floodwater coated grey-brown, the upper stonework areas were of clean red worn sandstone, the layers of their formation mirroring the nearby cliff. On the Holt side we strolled under the bridge, one of the arches conceals a path which had a mud-coated kissing gate, the use of which just a few weeks before,

would have required scuba diving equipment. An interpretation board gives the earliest record of a bridge here as 1338, while a description from 1627 mentions a bridge of ten arches, "upon the fifth arch from Holt stands a tower or gatehouse". An 18th century sketch shows the tollgate tower, while a painting dated 1793 is also reproduced showing a man on horseback proceeding toward the former tower, by then just a stump.

J. S. Howson comments how the bridge 'in combination with the low cliff... is a most pleasing object in the landscape' and how it narrowly escaped demolition 'and we may congratulate all lovers of the picturesque that the county authorities on one side of the stream could not agree with the county authorities on the other'.

Up the hill we came to the warm and welcoming river-echoed church of Holt, also called St. Chads (I cannot see that causing any confusion). There are more signs of the civil war here, in an ancient door, three loopholes, said to have been used to poke muskets out of, have been plugged.

The search for Mabon ap Modron
The Ouzel of Cilgwri guided the searchers to the Stag of Rhedynfre (Holt*) who told them he had not heard of Mabon, but would be their guide to an animal older than he...

(*The stories collectively known as the 'Mabinogion' are among the finest flowerings of Celtic brilliance and are thought to date back to the eleventh century, the story of Culhwch and Olwen is earlier still, with subject matter contemporary perhaps with the dawn of the Celtic world. Myths become legends and folktales, Gods become identifiable characters and the Otherworld is given form in the landscape. The modern place names which are marked with an asterisk are taken from 'Myths and Legends of Llangollen and the Dee Valley').

St. Chads (Farndon) told her tale through a beautifully illustrated leaflet, while St, Chads (Holt) has numerous interpretation boards which give the history of the church, the bridge, the castle, and daily life in times gone by. An "outstanding example of a medieval parish church and is a grade II listed building," ... "Close to the modern town lies the site of one of the more unusual elements of the Roman military takeover of Britain. It is known as a works depot and covered an area of around 20 acres. Excavations have revealed buildings where pottery, and roof tiles and other building materials such as hypocausts and water pipes were made... the kilns were excavated, nine in all... nothing is visible today... but in 1991 after ploughing a large fragment of Roman brick was found on which were incised the names of three workmen and their expenses or wages".

From the grounds of the church her namesake is visible on the opposite bank, the shimmering white blossom of apple trees was fragrant and popular with bees. Swallows flew above us, our first and very welcome sighting of the season, orange tipped butterflies regaled us. The ancient and ornate south door with its Tudor arch and coats of arms, faces the castle gate but is no longer used.

In the centre of the village the trunk of the late medieval market cross was re-set

in 1896 on top of a series of steps, the lower one is curved, possibly by the erosive effect of centuries of human buttocks. A shady leaf strewn path led us to the castle, it was not my first visit, even so it seemed a surprising way to arrive at a castle, sandwiched quietly between river and village.

John de Warenne, a man best avoided on bridges, built the five-sided castle around 1283–1308 to control his newly acquired marcher lordship of Bromfield and Yale. An interpretation board tells that Richard II was so impressed by the security of the castle that he made it his treasury. The first sight of the castle gives little impression of this strength, we were looking at a hill, around which a deep ditch leads to sheer quarried faces, (now topped by houses), an easy point from which to attack the main castle? It's not until the modern metal walkway is ascended onto the hilltop that it becomes apparent that all that remains of the castle is at floor level, which sits on top of the plinth which was left when the surrounding stone was quarried out. The castle would have towered over the bordering country and been the highest structure visible for miles. It would have been within a palisade extending to Castle Street in the modern-day village and managed to resist attacks in the Owain Glyndŵr uprising when Wrexham and Hawarden fell.

When the Lordship was granted to Sir William Stanley, his wealth allowed refurbishment of the castle, though he did not enjoy it for long, in 1495 Henry VII had him executed for treason for his part in a conspiracy. The castle fell into decay but was patched up during the civil war, surrendering to the Parliamentarians in 1647 after an eleven-month siege. It was subsequently dismantled, the stone being carried away both for local use, but also further field, particularly by boat, for Sir Thomas Grosvenor's new hall at Eaton.

The moat here still sometimes floods in winter, although on our visit the water lapped gently past us around fifteen feet below the top of the banks, a tranquil scene from where we could see and hear the traffic on the Wrexham to Nantwich road, freely passing the former mighty control point.

We walked under the under the flyover, noticing the "Welcome to Wales" sign as we glanced back. The fields were being ploughed by farmers who I am sure were grateful for some dry weather after the long-wet winter which hadn't quite released her grip from the field edges. I was glad I had not put my winter boots away just yet, the turned earth was dark and loamy, a rich alluvial flood plain. Three shrill-calling buzzards made lazy circles above us, then to our surprise two oystercatchers peeped straight and true above our heads. Dog walkers from Holt faded into the distance, we soon had the landscape and long river windings to ourselves. There were no bank holiday traffic jams here, spring birdsong filled the air, Wrexham industrial estate sat incongruously on a low hill overlooking a time-slowed rustic setting.

A single oak stood forlorn in the middle of a large open field, a fairy tree gateway to the underworld. At a delicious bend in the river, we took up the shade kindly offered by a willow tree and picnicked on cooling watermelon on what

The Holy Dee

was to be the warmest May Day holiday since it was introduced. Hover flies were all about but did not bother us, lambs ran to their mothers as we passed. The map showed three consecutive border loops away from the river, presumably where the course of the river has drifted east over the years, forming ox bow lakes, and taking the path of least resistance.

From a shady vantage point, we watched a goosander with seven gorgeous balls of fluff chicks hurry away from us. We were treated to the sight and sound of sand martins as they twisted and swooped, before disappearing into their nest tunnels in high mud banks.

Nearing Old Hall, a hare sprang up from his form as we were almost on top of him, his cover blown, he sprinted to the edge of the field where he sat proud on his haunches, brown tipped ears to the sky and watched us pass.

1. Holt Castle; 2. Lowland riverbank

7. Maelor Saesneg

At one of the many bends here, as the Dee carves its sinuous path, the border once more takes leave of our company, as it takes off to the south and then east resuming its southerly path about a mile from the outskirts of Whitchurch. At Welsh End it takes a westerly course, capturing Bettisfield in an icing bag loop before resuming westward to re-join the bright open reaches of the Dee upstream of Erbistock.

I Have always loved maps. When I was young, I had a mug with a map of Wales printed on it. I would often pause mid-tea to inspect it, to dream of the far-off places marked on it, like Llangollen, Aberystwyth, and St. David's. One bit which often puzzled me was an area marked "Part of Flints." Which was separated from the rest of Flintshire by Denbighshire, and I do believe we are now looking at it.

'Maelor' originated as a Cantref (hundred) of the Kingdom of Powys based on Bangor is y coed. It became divided from the rest of the Kingdom around the eighth century when it fell under the Kingdom of Mercia, to be later reclaimed for Powys by Madog ap Maredudd. When he died in 1160, the Kingdom was subdivided amongst his heirs. By the thirteenth century Maelor included Maelor Gymraeg (Welsh Maelor) west of the Dee based upon Wrexham, and Maelor Saesneg (English Maelor) to the east of the Dee which included various Anglo-Norman lordships. In 1536 it was included in the newly created county of Flintshire. Although part of Flintshire, it was an exclave, surrounded by Cheshire, Shropshire, and Denbighshire, often referred to as Flintshire Detached. J. S. Howson describes it wonderfully as "a detached portion of the former county being thrown over the latter, like a great boulder disjointed from the mountains".

Events in Maelor Saesneg have had a huge influence in Wales. Owain Glyndŵr was raised by his foster father Sir David Hanmer in the settlement of the same name, while R.S. Thomas, one of our finest poets, was curate and would find his voice as "his innocence would disappear in the frying-pan of the 1940s" while watching and hearing from the vicarage door at

Tallarn (Tallwrn) Green, the German planes flying over to drop their bombs on Liverpool docks.

It is great to resolve the mystery of the mug, to see the part of Flintshire which I had imagined having floated off into neighbouring counties. Sadly, it is no longer referred to as Flintshire detached, it became part of Clwyd in 1974 and later part of Wrexham County Borough, where it continues to reside. I quite like the idea that it may one day go off on its travels again.

Approaching the confluence with the Clywedog, overgrown flood embankments diverted us from the water's edge. Through a gap in the undergrowth, we glimpsed a goosander taking advantage of the cover, she spotted us straight away, making off with around a dozen chicks, a few on her back, the remainder fizzed along behind her. A sparrow hawk overhead added to their haste. The entrance to the Clywedog is guarded by a willow, there were otter prints in the soft mud around her base, a riverine motorway junction. In the distance we could see a bridge on private land at Pickhill Meadows, a crossing point teasingly with no access, a small part of a big story to sadly remain untold.

The Clywedog runs past the Wrexham industrial estate which is built on the site of a World War II Royal Ordnance Factory where up to 13,000 workers made cordite for use in shells. Michael Drayton in his epic landscape poem Poly-Olbion also made reference to industry as far back as the early 17th century, "*Out of the leaden Mines, then with her sullied face Claweddock casts about where Gwenrow shee may greet, Till like two loving friends they under Wrexam meet*".

The Clywedog planted a seed in our minds for a diversionary perambulation which we were to realize some time later when we followed the rich diversity of the Clywedog Valley Trail from those lead mines at Minera to King's Mill in the suburbs of Wrexham. It was a wonderful walk, through the beautiful Plas Power woods, past the Bersham Heritage Centre and across the splendour of Erddig Country Park. Wrexham is well worth another diversion to see the Perpendicular might of St. Giles' church, which dominates the town and was aptly described by Sir Simon Jenkins as 'the glory of the Marches'.

Nearing Bangor on Dee (Bangor is y

Coed) the twin sandstone abutments of an old railway line emerged like Mayan ruins out of the undergrowth. The Wrexham to Ellesmere line was closed in 1962, the forty-five-meter lattice bridge which spanned the Dee here was dismantled and carried away leaving the dressed stonework like the jaws of a stone monster waiting to pounce on some passing vessel.

Weeds trailed lazily in the flow, fish jumped clear of the water, mayflies drifted up from the surface. Long tailed tits flitted between the trees on the riverbank, iridescent blue and green damsel flies were all around us. As we entered a meadow with bird song echoing, we saw orange tipped butterflies canoodle amongst forget me knots and buttercups.

Spring was thick and sweet in the air; bees were in overdrive. A fire crest twitched from branch to branch.

The path runs along the top of a flood embankment, a sign on a tree for a local angling club has notices in eastern European languages noting that fishing is private. A kingfisher peeped its approach, a passer-by shared in the electric blue joy and told us they were nesting nearby upstream. A delicious sweep in the river had bites taken out of her banks by the flow.

As we neared the village walking through delicate willow groves, sand martins captivated us with a low-level aerial display as they twisted and turned with flashes of blue, white, black and grey. We heard music and soon arrived at the welcome sight of the Royal Oak which was heaving with tipplers taking advantage of the warm bank holiday weather. Inside the pub, a photo from 1910 shows flat capped men rowing coracles down the flooded high street. Bangor on Dee has been flooded many times – a scheme is now in place to divert flood waters away from the village, though storm Christoph in January 2021 raised the Dee to an unprecedented level, leading to flooding in the area and evacuations in the village. Natural Resources Wales reported that some of their gauges on the Dee registered record high levels.

We enjoyed cooling riverside refreshments in the sun, a genuine happy hour. On our visit in February, we were the only takers for the outdoor benches above the ice fronded extremities of the Dee. On that occasion we met two fishermen "Any

1. Orange tipped butterfly;
2. Lazy lowland river

luck?" I asked. "Not today." One of them proceeded to show us a picture on his phone of a 16 1/2lb pike, caught near the bridge. A whopper indeed. Howson saw a twenty-two-pound salmon caught here 'clean from the sea'. It was caught from a coracle; he went on to say that the coracle races held at Chester are almost always won by men from this neighbourhood.

The five-arched stone bridge which dates from about 1660, is believed to have been built by Inigo Jones, the approach road is at a 90-degree angle, depriving the unsuspecting traveller of a great view. The sharp bend has resulted in deep scratches in her stone walls which curve upwards and outwards. Metal staples are left prone on her weather worn top, her grooved cobbled surface rises upward to its centre to slowly reveal the pub on the opposite bank, a fantastic trick. The narrow crossing has alcove passing places, in one of which we stopped to watch a grey wagtail living up to its name around the pools at the river edge.

Opposite the Royal Oak, there is a beautiful stone war memorial, where a statue of the Virgin Mary on a pillar holding two wreaths leads easily to the church of St. Dunawd which is a gem. Low sun carried shards of colour from the stained-glass windows onto the dark walls.

An extensive bilingual history of the Church and the local area includes cabinets of local finds such as roman tiles from the church grounds while brother Duncisian of the wood surprised us, sat at his desk in his cowl. We learnt that Saint Florian is the patron saint of rivers and of a forthcoming cheese quiz at Overton scout hut, with a gourmet buffet.

As we exited, we saw a notice reminding visitors to close the door, stating how the birds are loved, so long as they are outside. In the eaves of the porch, an owl looked down at us, a plastic one. A happy church. In the churchyard, a squirrel ran through angled gravestones under a deep blue sky. The bridge was now bathed in sunlight, its stone a mixture of reds and yellows, running down to greys and green mosses near the water line.

This area was once dominated ecclesiastically by the monastery of Bangor, a great centre of learning which was established by St. Dunawd. In around c.613-616, when the pagan forces of Aethelfrith of Northumbria arrived, the monks supported the army of Powys, calling for divine intervention and offering

no resistance as they were cut down. According to Bede, twelve hundred monks were slaughtered and only fifty escaped with their lives. Victory gave another step westward for the Anglo-Saxon's in the cleaving of the Britons of Strathclyde, Rheged and Elmet in the Old North or Hen Ogledd of Taliesin, from those in Wales.

Sir Walter Scott commemorated the event in poetry.

"High their holy anthem sounds,
Cestria's vale the hymn rebounds,
Floating down the silvan Dee...

Slaughtered down by heathen blade,
Bangor's peaceful monks are laid."

At Basingwerk we saw a monastery which stood for hundreds of years on the banks of the Holy Dee, before being razed into a picturesque ruin. At Chester we saw a monastery re-purposed as a cathedral and friaries pulled down, their sites built over by the interests of commerce, but their locations living on in the street names. Here, no trace of the ruined monastery remains, Scott's poem told of how "Long thy ruins told the tale, shattered towers and broken arch" but their location remains unknown, the second great religious house to have disappeared in this short lowland section of the river. At Poulton, it seems likely that the site of the abbey may have been established, but at Bangor on Dee, some believe that the ruins may lie under the present course of the deified river, which for now at least is content to keep her secret. A future twist in her sinuous path may yet reveal her ruins, to the delight archaeologists, artists, and poets.

There was no footpath on the eastern side of the river from where I might view the racecourse and re-live the afternoon when I watched a horse which I had backed gallop to the front of the field, prompting thoughts of a stylish new jacket from one of the course-side country gent outfitters, only for it to be forced off its winning line by a riderless horse, allowing the rest of the field to canter past.

The course sits in a C-shaped loop of the meandering river, there are records of it going from being dry, to under seven feet of water in just five hours. In 1402 an English army camped on the eastern side of the Dee in the vicinity of Bangor on Dee, in preparation for an attack on Owain Glyndŵr's men. The wind whipped up Llyn Tegid at Bala, causing the river to surge downstream and drown many of the soldiers in their tents. Spirits had been summoned from the vasty deep.

Continuing south, my map showed several paths leading down through open farmland toward the river; to reach it, however, would first involve the completion of a series of krypton factor like tests. The footpath signs were sometimes covert, gate number one was secured by a loop of rope over a post which was so tight that it had to be eased up, a millimetre or so at a time, until it could eventually be heaved over the top. Gate number two had a piece of wood on a length of rope attached to a further length of chain with a padlock attached to it, that had to be fed through the supporting ironwork to allow it to open. It was however the gate of a thousand knots which finally beat our mental stamina into submission and took us into the physical stage of the test which we completed with an inelegant up and over. After regathering our strength and composure, we dusted ourselves down, and continued down a steep catkin covered path, still slippery after the previous night's thunderstorm showers to arrive victorious at the chocolate brown surging silty river. We were soon rewarded with an open landscape, a gorgeous natural amphitheatre, a flood plain bowl in which cows laid down and munched lazily as we passed.

We entered a wood of tall straight poplars, which slowed and calmed us, a further prize for negotiating the puzzle path. It was like being in a zen garden, there was soft stippled sunlight on a palette of greens, the colour which psychiatrists say relaxes us, reminding us of our deep time connection with the forests. Lilting birdsong carried across to where we stood on a curve of the path on to the very edge of the riverbank and mingled with the soothing sound of water flowing over tree trunks. A pair of technicolour mandarin ducks and a shimmer of metallic blue damsel flies contrasted against the brown of the river. The smell of wild garlic was mild and soothing, the previous wood had head circling insects aplenty, here they called a truce. As the poplars gave way to broad leaves, a woodpecker called, but did not knock. We moved on with many pauses, in a walking meditation. I do not know how long it took to traverse the wood; I am not sure it could be measured in real-time.

We emerged once more into the open, a large crack willow drew us to her, where we cosied under her sunshield canopy. A female chaffinch landed on a fallen trunk directly in front of us and was soon joined by a brightly coloured male who faced her and performed a hopping dance to the left and right, a kind of bouncy line dance. He flew up and gave an excellent demonstration of what the birds and the bees do naturally. The female stared ahead, possibly wondering what was for tea while the male repeated the highly acrobatic and energetic coupling six times. If I'd had a couple of those score cards which show points awarded to ice skating contestants, it would have been a double ten from me. My map identified this area as "Nant y Lladron," valley of thieves. We passed unhindered, sweet times.

At Overton bridge, the very welcome sight of the Cross Foxes Inn was a wonderful stop for refreshments. Dating back to 1748, it was built for local estate workers, and became a stopping point for stagecoaches travelling from Shrewsbury to Chester. From her beer garden we appreciated the double arches of the red sandstone bridge and quietly toasted the people who toiled to make it, so that we could cross the deep valley with ease. The flood plain is now behind us.

Continuing alone, I followed the Wat's Dyke path from the bridge along the edge of a tree lined field on eastern side of the river. On hearing a kerfuffle in the high Branches, I paused and was amply rewarded by the sight of a greater spotted woodpecker, brilliant in white and black and red moving from tree to tree no doubt hunting to feed nearby chicks. I soon heard the heavy sound of cascading water and saw flashes of white through the leaves. A large weir soon became visible, over which water cascaded noisily to produce the foamy flow which had quizzed us the day before and as we sat outside the downstream inn. The lower walls of Erbistock Mill are formed with large sandstones blocks, which become progressively smaller toward the top of the building, the top third of this substantial building is brick. The remains of a water wheel lie at her side. Below the weir a fly fisherman flicked coils of yellow line across the flow. I had not walked far, but this was a view which could not be quickly passed, I sat a while to soak it in.

Further along the path, the air was full

Erbistock weir

of sweet-smelling summer nectar, the sound of the weir was gradually replaced by birdsong. At Quarry Wood, straight rock faces could well identify where the mill's sandstone walls were sourced, a local supply. At a straight section of path, a pine tree had fallen across at waist height, perfectly round and bare of bark, the theme tune of the horse of the year show entered my head, I considered running and gracefully clearing it, before taking stock of my athletic abilities and bending with a groan as I eased under it.

The river flow widened and slowed, held up by the weir. In the following field a post was marked with the flood level of the 9th of February 1946, the same date as on the plaque I had seen near Eaton Hall. The marker was at my eye level, it is probably not often seen in this quiet corner of a remote field, but on a benign summer's day, it was another powerful reminder of the power of the Dee. Nearby cows were also thankful, the now slightly angled memorial seemed to have been used as a convenient rubbing post. A loud thrum caused me to look up, I expected to see a helicopter overhead, but there was none, the noise was repeated as I passed each fresh cow pat and a swarm of flies, natures mini helicopters, became airborne.

The course of the river took its last, long lazy curve to the east before she assumes her broadly east-west demeanour from here to her source. At the apex of the arc, I met the only other people that I would come across taking advantage of this quiet stretch, a group of bleary-eyed young lads packing away their camping equipment after a Tom Sawyer style night in the open air on the bank.

I welcomed the Maelor Way as it joined me, running through an open swathe in the wheat from my left, cutting across the flatness of the flood plain field which extended to the surrounding amphitheatre hills. The Maelor Way extends for 24 miles from Grindley Brook near Whitchurch to Bronygarth in the shadow of Chirk Castle and would be a welcome companion for a few miles. Llan-y-cefn wood is broad leafed and sliced by numerous streams running off the hill. Near one of the wooden pallet style foot bridges, I glimpsed what looked like a squirrel, which disappeared beneath it, rather than heading upward, I have mistaken stoats in this manner before. I loitered a while but whatever it was remained stealthy. Fern fronded, dripping dark recesses in the sandstone escarpment on my left contrasted with the open sun dappled river on my right. The riparian hamlet of Erbistock with its sandstone church and cottage style Boat Inn bathed by sunlight looked very contented. I stood on the modern looking small concrete jetty and could see the winding drum above a V-shaped cut out for the ferry which once operated here. The doors were open, guests were arriving and taking seats in the sun-drenched garden. This was both pleasure and pain, a gorgeous view, on a hot summer's day, I looked about me for any remains of the old winching system which could be cobbled together for a Professor Heinz Wolff style great beer race crossing, but sadly I had to continue on my way unquenched.

I made a subsequent winter visit to Erbistock with a friend for a short winter walk upstream. St. Hilary's church was sadly locked, but we managed to console ourselves with a pint of IPA supped at the water's edge from the pub which was very much open and accessible on foot. We learnt that it dates to the 17th century and, at the time of our visit, there was a plan to restore the hand-operated chain ferry. Hopefully, the plan will survive the Covid-19 shock wave.

At Manley Hall weir, there is a gauging station for the Dee Regulation System which we will come across later.

On a small bluff with open views across the river, a tiny art-bench has been built against the base of a tall fir tree, placed by some benevolent soul, and very much appreciated. I missed Sophia's eyes as bird's landed nearby and were off again

The Boat at Erbistock

before I could focus my binoculars. I took in the peace, amazed that there was no queue for this perfectly placed bench in its glorious solitude. I heard a cough from across the bank, seeing the gravel spit devoid of fisherman I was puzzled, a while later I saw a figure walking, a check of my map showed that I was looking from Wat's Dyke Way to Wat's Dyke Way which runs downstream to Overton Bridge and back again, and why not, this is beautiful landscape in an area of few crossings, good enough to walk twice on any route.

1. A pilgrim's rest; 2. White swan

To the sound of grunting swans and calling moorhens I continued over a footbridge which made this walk international. I did not see a signpost, but I had just crossed from Wales into England, which was an odd feeling going west. A little further on a Shropshire Council path marker confirmed I had made the stealthy border crossing and Maelor Saesneg had slipped into the last reach of England to the banks of the Dee. Wrexham gave way to Shropshire, but nevertheless the names of the hills, historic farmhouses and woods on my maps stubbornly remained in the old language as Penybryn, Plas-yn-y- coed and Coed yr Allt carried my eyes at least, back into Wales.

At a slope prickled with hawthorn trees, the path was lost among the criss-crossed churnings of bovine highways. The prospect was one of deep hoof imprints in the mud which was stained red from the underlying sandstone and interspersed with a few pristine green topped grassy islands. Stretching my foot onto the first stop of my planned island-hopping traverse, the plan began to unravel as the island collapsed into the goo. Island number two was similarly non-compliant with my plan, I was now knee-deep, times two, and praying that the herd did not come charging into the scene in a springtime frolic. A fall now would be very messy, I paused for a second, a thought momentarily crossed my mind that I could be sucked down here, never to found, mud fodder. With an almighty effort I schlooped my way across the morass to emerge into a field, dripping with bright orange mud from the knees down, the cows which were sat on the top of the bank stood up and stared, looking slightly sad to have missed out on the full feast of entertainment.

The path comes to an end at a lane which leads down to a water treatment plant. Not wishing to return to Overton bridge via cow-field Glastonbury I decided to walk up the lane to the main road and back to my car via Overton village. I cleaned my boots as best as I could in the grassy verges as I hitch-hiked along the road hoping for a lift, but realising success would be unlikely, as it looked like I'd gone through some sort of Maasai initiation ceremony. Plan B was to catch a bus, should one appear but alas rural buses are now on the endangered species list. So, I returned on Shanks's pony, on a baking hot day, kicking curls of mud into the air off my boots and finding time to take in the fantastic yew trees at Overton Church en route.

For the next few miles, the river and public footpaths are not in harmony, I could see no green or red dashed lines to be explored, no landscape to be mind-travelled in advance. But then, I fortuitously picked up a leaflet for the

Wrexham walking festival which included a five-mile circular walk from Chirk taking in "rivers meet" at the confluence of the Dee and Ceiriog. An opportunity indeed, available at the exact time as our undertaking reached this area. Serendipity had delivered a stroke of luck.

On an early June evening, the group set out along the last stage of the Ceiriog, which retained the beauty of its valley to the last. I ascended the stone arch of Pont y blew, so that at its centre I had one foot in England and one in Wales, for the border leaves the Dee at our destination and follows the Ceiriog. From here on upstream, the Dee resides firmly in Wales, the mother country. The final stretch of our walk was over private land, which the walk leaders had kindly gained permission to enter. The confluence crept up on me unexpectedly, the Ceiriog flowing in at an opposing angle to the Dee, her waters forming an 'S' shaped swirl as they diffused into the greater flow.

The points where two or more rivers meet are auspicious to Hindus, the ashes of loved ones are often scattered at such places, so that the soul can be liberated from this world in several directions. This certainly felt like a highly auspicious place, a glorious spot on the Holy river to sit and rest and contemplate for a while.

During the walk we came to several huge old oaks, at one of which, a cohort of fellow ramblers spontaneously joined outstretched hands to circle her ancient trunk. Oaks continue to enchant us, druids practised rituals in oak groves and cherished the mistletoe that grows in oak-tree Branches. The connection continues in landscape and language, the Welsh word for oaks is derw, while that for druid is derwydd. The oaks we came across reminded me of 'the Crogen Oak' located just a few miles higher up the Ceiriog Valley, which David Lloyd George described as "A little bit of heaven on earth". An unmissable diversion.

At the bottom of the Chirk Castle estate, where Offa's Dyke runs down to the valley floor, a wooden board in front of the tree identifies it as "The Oak at the Gate of the Dead – Derwen Adwy'r Meirwon, (11th century)" which would mean it would have been standing and is possibly the last living witness to the Battle of Crogen in 1165.

Interpretation boards nearby tell of increasing hostility between the princes of Wales and the English crown which led to Henry II's army of over 30,000 soldiers invading with the aim of 'the total annihilation of the Welsh race'. A coalition of Welsh princes, for once amalgamated under the leadership of Owain Gwynedd ambushed the army at Offa's Dyke. As Henry's army tried to force their way through a gap in the dyke, thousands of arrows rained down on them, eventually the overwhelming numbers forced their way through although suffering huge losses. The invasion would go on to fail in the wilds of the Berwyn mountains due to sustained Welsh guerrilla tactics and atrocious weather conditions. Henry II, probably the greatest monarch in medieval Europe never tried to conquer Wales again, independence would survive for nearly another 120 years.

I read once that an oak tree lasts for around 900 years, taking 300 years to grow, 300 years to live and 300 years to die. The Crogen Oak has been split in two by the ravages of weather and time, the old trunks are splayed out as if crawling along the valley floor, but amidst the bleached trunks new shoots reach upward, the old oak will hopefully hang on to tell its tale for a long time yet.

Upstream of 'rivers meet' my map shows the riverbanks to be mostly heavily wooded. I have often driven on the A483 viaduct and stolen glimpses of the valley on either side, wondering if there are any footpaths below. It would seem not, my daydreams have been futile, a reverie ending in a cul-de-sac, but my loss is presumably wildlife's gain. I am sure a side-on view of the viaduct would be mighty impressive, containing some 30,000 tonnes of concrete, it is 348m long and stands 57m above river level. Opened in 1990 she is the most modern of several hugely impressive crossings which straddle the Dee valley in the next few miles.

Jim Perrin, more adventurous and combative than I, records in his wonderful Borrowvian 'River Map,' a pilgrimage along the Dee, walking along this stretch at the turn of the millennium, he described the scene at that time of 'clear-felled conifers – the ground around us in ruins – of a place that no one now knows that was eerily and unnaturally lifeless'. It was not always so; I went on to read J.S. Howson's account of a view in this area as "on the whole the most remarkable view in the whole course of the Dee". A woodcut drawing shows 'Nant-y-Belan, Wynnestay Park' with two men (possibly the authors) in conversation as they admire the vista of the Dee flowing down through the Vale of Llangollen with the Berwyn mountains beyond. They identify this as not only being at the southernmost point of the park of Sir Watkin Williams-Wynn, but also as being one of the two extremities of the lowland region of the Dee which 'may be defined by the palatial residences of Wynnestay and Eaton'. They describe 'the presence of the long line of arches of the great railway viaduct in much strength and grandeur, seen suddenly through the foliage among which we were wandering'. The view 'is obtained from terraced height above the river, this viaduct is one element, and the aqueduct also, slightly beyond. But the great feature of the view is the outspread beauty of the woods, among which the stream is embosomed'.

They go on to describe 'what seemed like an apparition from the time of the ancient Britons, when they met 'two men with coracles on their backs, returning towards Overton from a fishing expedition, apparently not very successful, higher up the river'.

Howson was not the first to be beguiled by the view, in 1770 Richard Wilson was commissioned by Sir Watkin Williams-Wynn to paint the vista from his estate, and a few years later Thomas Pennant described how it 'merits a visit from every traveller ... a magnificent view of the Dee, rolling awefully in a deep chasm ringed by woods'.

The name of the Williams-Wynn family kept cropping up as I progressed along the river, I later returned to this area to see an exhibition at St. Mary's church in Ruabon, one of the finest Churches in north east Wales. This was my first acquaintance with Ruabon, where I am pleased to report that I did not come across any of the miners who George Borrow was warned would knock him to the ground. I found a peaceful village of warm-stoned houses and dozing window cats.

The search for Mabon ap Modron
The Stag of Rhedynfre brought them to the Grey Owl of Cwm Cawlwyd (Ruabon/Rhiw Mabon*) who told them he

had not heard of Mabon, but would be their guide to a place where the oldest creature lived who had been further afield than he ...
(* See earlier note re the Mabinogion)

The exhibition illustrated the history of Ruabon village and 'the Williams-Wynn family of Wynnstay Hall'. A section of the beautifully illustrated Church guidebook gave a fascinating overview of how the fortunes of the house of Wynnstay were established after the civil war by Sir William Williams, who descended from a tenth-century Lord of Anglesey. A successful lawyer and elected speaker of the House of Commons, the guidebook goes on to detail the joining of two families and how 'luck, astute management and marriage alliance brought the Williams-Wynn family from the comparative obscurity of an Anglesey rectory to make them leaders of the North Wales gentry'. By the early eighteenth-century Watkin Williams-Wynn had come into possession of over a hundred thousand acres.

The estate, standing on the plateau above the Dee valley was first known as Watstay, after Wat's Dyke which runs through the estate. The first house was probably built by William Eyton around 1616. A fire in 1858 resulted in almost complete rebuilding of the house for the sixth baronet, in stone in French Renaissance chateau style. Heavy death duties caused the Williams-Wynn family to leave Wynnstay in the 1940s, severing a link of over two centuries with Ruabon. The 'palatial residence' became a private school known as Lindisfarne until 1994 and is now converted into apartments.

Should the viewpoint at Nant-y Belan still be accessible in the thick woods, the remarkable views which have been described would now include the A483 viaduct, the hurly-burly of modern traffic could well be a distraction and a test on the ears. On the western side of the new road at Newbridge a powerful and impressive grey stone lodge is signed as the 'Wynnstay Lodge and Park private land – no access'. The lodge was built in the 1820s and is thought to be one of the finest in Britain. The spear-headed cast-iron gates were closed, washing was hung from a line which stretched across the driveway, time rolls on in the Dee valley.

8. To the stream in the sky – Cymru – Y Dyfrdwy

Upstream of the A483, the river follows a gloriously inefficient loop in the shape of a bird's head around a steep hill. The tall bridge at Newbridge/Cefn is thought to be the fifth on the site, the engineer responsible is sadly not celebrated on the structure. An interpretation board in the village itself gives some history, the first recorded bridge here was built in 1392/1393 replacing the slow ferry. The base of a pillar of one of the earlier bridges can be seen upstream, sitting in the flow like a petrified boat. Richard Wilson's painting from the 1770s shows a substantial bridge here.

Walking up the hill, the impressive nineteen arches of Cefn Viaduct came into view. A lane under the railway line brought me to Tŷ Mawr country park, which occupies a glorious area extending from beneath the viaduct along the Dee. I called in at the welcoming visitor centre for an ice cream to try and reduce my core temperature on what was a piping hot June day. I also picked up a couple of booklets detailing walks in the area, one of which informed me that the viaduct which dominates the park is 45 metres high and 460 metres long and was built using local Cefn sandstone by Henry Robertson. The first train to cross broke down, forcing the dignitaries on board to spend an uncomfortable night on board before being rescued.

My booklets and indeed my route there showed the Cefn Mawr area to be marked with the history of the industrial revolution, there are disused rail and tram

1. The Cefn Viaducte; 2. Aqueduct ahoy;
3. The Stream in the sky

The Cefn Viaduct from the riverbank

lines, signs of collieries, foundries and the chemical works which operated until very recently, the scars of back-breaking toil remain.

George Borrow wrote of his walk from Llangollen to Wrexham and back "It was now quite night, and it would have been pitchy-dark but for the glare of forges. There was an immense glare to the south-west, which I conceived proceeded from those of Cefn Mawr. It lighted up the south-western sky: then there were two other glares nearer to me ... I struck across the fields and should probably have tumbled half-a-dozen times over pales and the like, but for the light of the Cefn furnaces before me which cast their red glow upon my path. I debouched upon the

Llangollen road near to the tramway leading up to the collieries. Two enormous sheets of flame shot up high into the air from the ovens, illumuning two spectral chimneys as high as steeples, also smoky buildings, and grimy figures moving about. There was a clanging of engines, a noise of shovels and a falling of coals truly horrible. The glare was so great that I could distinctly see the minutest lines upon my hand. Advancing along the tramway I obtained a nearer view of the hellish buildings, the chimneys, the demoniac figures".

The backdrop to my walk was far more benign, the path along the Dee, overlooked by the Viaduct was a scene of post-industrial tranquillity. There was a full boisterous flow despite the dry period which was being experienced, damsel flies frolicked in sun dappled groves on the tree lined banks, a family of Canada geese convoyed under a clear blue sky.

I stopped for a foot-cooling paddle, a man sat on a nearby shady bench dozed and nodded into and out of a book.

I took out my map which showed Offa's Dyke, that huge Mercian slash in the landscape extending between seas, a message to the Princes of Powys, running down through the covering of trees on the opposite bank. An out of place, mortal marker of former times alongside this quiet stretch of water. The Dyke is the largest linear earthwork in Britain and a scheduled monument. When originally constructed it is thought to have measured 8 metres from the ditch bottom to the bank top. It is almost as if Offa was trying to cut right through the land, to be rid of the troublesome Welsh, the indigenous inhabitants, the *Welisc*, or foreigners. If he had kept on digging, Wales might have drifted off into the Irish sea and have been marked on my old mug as 'Part of Brit. (detached)'.

The modern border and the dykes now lie behind us, I continued along the Afon Dyfrdwy to a sandy curve, known locally as the beach, where teenagers swam, just beyond the no swimming signs. The path upstream sat under the curve of the trees like an arboreal wave which offered welcome shade. A multi-tasking jogger passed me, sporting outsize headphones to blot out the sound of water tumbling over stones and the sweet soothing song of a blackbird.

The horizontal iron lines of Pontcysyllte aqueduct appeared high above the trees, although I knew it was coming up, it was a surprise to see it where I scanned for a calling buzzard. The song of the river became stronger as it flowed through the steepening tree-lined valley, its waters glinted in the strong sunlight, natural stone piers rose vertically between the trees in a defiant and poetic act of negative geotropism.

It felt odd walking up a steep path from a river to a canal, but there it was, the 'stream in the sky', high above the valley floor. Stream is an apt description since there was a noticeable flow of water through its iron banks. Silver flashing fish were visible, rising to the surface for morsels of food, I wondered if they would be prone to vertigo if they were aware of their lofty circumstances as unwitting members of an aquatic extreme sports society.

Sophia joined me to merge with the walkers going over the aqueduct, who number over 200,000 a year, I pondered if we would suffer the "Pendro" or dizziness which affected Borrows guide, John Jones, despite him having previously worked as a mountain shepherd. Some walkers held on to the rails, others leaned over to confirm if the stone arches are in as straight a line now as they were over 200 years ago. They are.

We took Michael Faraday's advice that this is 'too grand a thing to be hastily passed' and dawdled a while as canal boats crept past, some of the occupants of which were peering warily over the edge of the trough down to the tumbling waters below. Upstream the warm stoned seventeenth century 'Roman Bridge', Pont Cysyllte sat in a tree-lined sun-bathed river hollow, looking glad to have had

some traffic taken away from it.

The stone piers taper upward and are hollow in their upper stages to reduce weight on the foundations, they support the cast iron trough which is held in place by lugs and weight of the water. It is a truly graceful design of the highest quality which complements the surrounding landscape and has become home to much local wildlife. It underwent a restoration in 2003–2004, a wonderful account of the project and the dedication of the team who carried it out is recorded in a book by Richard J Turner-Thomas who recalls a fish rescue operation that was mounted after she was drained overnight to reveal roach, dace, bullheads, perch, and a single pike approximately ten pound in weight. He goes on to record that tawny and little owls have been observed in the inspection holes in the piers, while pipistrelle bats had to be tickled out of their roosts and relocated to other piers by an environmental officer as the work progressed. In the summer months swifts' nest on the stonework shelves.

At its southern end a huge man-made embankment, possibly the largest civil earthworks of the eighteenth century in Britain, carries the canal to the village of Froncysyllte from where we returned, as did Borrow, at the request of his guide, along the road over the Roman Bridge where vehicles must wait their turn at the traffic lights and crick necked pedestrians must reciprocate while tucked in the packhorse style triangular recesses.

Arriving back at the basin, gongoozlers leaned on railings and ice cream carrying visitors walked alongside holiday boats which were being prepared for onward journeys. We crossed over the swing bridge in front of the dry dock, to the Visitor Centre which is in an old workshop and gives a great overview, not only of the aqueduct but of the complete eleven-mile linear corridor of the Llangollen canal which forms the UNESCO World Heritage Site (WHS) which runs from Llantisilio to Gledrid Bridge in Shropshire, it is the first WHS in the UK to straddle two countries.

We learnt that the aqueduct, at 127 feet, is as tall as nine double decker buses piled on top of each other and is the highest navigable aqueduct in the world and the longest in the UK. It is internationally recognised as a

The Aqueduct

masterpiece of civil engineering, comprising 18 stone pillars and 19 arches, which took 10 years to construct from 1795 to 1805. The trough of iron plates holds 1.5 million litres of water, is 1,000ft long and the joints were sealed with welsh flannel. The aqueduct was the work of many outstanding figures including, among many others, Thomas Telford who was 'General Agent, Surveyor, architect and overlooker for the Works', William Jessop who was the consulting engineer and William Hazeldine who was the ironmaster. A computer-generated display of the building of the aqueduct shows the coffer dams being erected and the piers being built up from the riverbed using stone delivered by a tramway down the steep valley side. The tramways extended onto platforms which supplied the increasing height of the piers as they gradually progressed skyward.

While the Pontcysyllte Aqueduct is the jewel in the crown of the WHS, it contains many other innovative features such as the first tunnel in the U.K. to have a towpath, this leads to the aqueduct at Chirk which straddles the England-Wales border in appealing parallel with the railway viaduct. The canal was built with precision across steep slopes and valleys along a remarkably direct route that does not need a single lock within the WHS.

But why go to the trouble and expense of taking a canal across the hills and through the ether for a high-level ride above the Dee in such an audacious manner? The whole of the Ellesmere canal cost some £500,000, a huge amount of money at that time. In the latter years of the eighteenth century the industrial revolution was in full swing, industrialists in the Ruabon area were seeking a way of transporting coal, iron ore, clay, slate, limestone, and finished products to wider markets. In the era of canal mania, a project was conceived to join the rivers Mersey, Dee, and Severn via a canal which would run from Shrewsbury, past Ellesmere, from which it would take its original name, to Ruabon, and on to Chester before reaching the Mersey at the new Ellesmere Port.

Work on the aqueduct was well under way when it was announced that the plan for the continuation of the canal across the northern coalfield through Ruabon was to be abandoned. The expense and risks involved in negotiating the higher ground, which would have involved

digging a tunnel, possibly longer than anything built before, coupled with finding a reliable water supply on the high ground were too great. A decision was made that the canal would take the route through Shropshire to join the Chester Canal.

A short extension was built to a pair of docks which served the industrialist Exuperius Pickering's limekilns (a name surely due for a comeback), while the Plas Kynaston Canal went a stage further, extending towards Cefn Mawr to access the Plas Kynaston iron foundry, which cast most of the ironwork for the aqueduct, as well as a coal mine, a pottery, and a chemical works. This extension unfortunately now lies buried, I picked up a local newspaper in the Telford Inn, formerly Scotch hall, which was built for the supervising engineer, which reported ambitious plans to reopen it. The planned northward route from Pontcysyllte would go no further, save for an isolated two-mile section of a Branch line which was dug near Ffrwd, in eager anticipation of the receipt of water and the task of carrying of freight, which sadly, did not happen. Canal mania was nearing its end, given different circumstances I have no doubt that team Telford would have completed the route as planned to cross the Dee once more and connect with the section of the canal which was built from Chester to its terminus at Ellesmere Port. I am sure that it would have been done in a furtherance of the grace and style of what is now known as the Llangollen canal and it would have the longevity to give the modern-day visitor one more reason to visit Chester.

The abandonment of the northern route meant a new source of water was required for the Ellesmere Canal. In 1808 the canal was extended upstream of Llangollen, to the Dee at Llantysilio, there Telford designed a weir, which guided water into the 'feeder' canal.

The canal was last used for commerce in the 1930s by which time rail and road transport had effectively made most of the canal network redundant. It is hard for me to believe that the aqueduct at that time was in danger of being demolished. Campaigns were launched to save the canal, but a major factor in its continued existence was the fact that it was by then carrying a large quantity of drinking water through the network to supply the north west of England, so Pontcysyllte was also saved by English thirst for Welsh water.

I took a last look at the canal boats being carried on their way over the aqueduct by the late-to-the-party waters of the Llangollen canal, reflecting that what is now part of a WHS, was once almost demolished, before leaving Trevor Basin, the name of which always makes me think of a nickname for a local plumber.

My map showed no footpaths along the Dee to Llangollen, but no matter, an excellent alternative is available, the WHS canal towpath doubles as a convenient and highly scenic cycle way. As the canal is fed from the Dee, which sparkled and snaked some distance below the path, I convinced myself that I was following her waters if not her exact course.

I think this was possibly the only time in my life that my human effort was faster than mechanised power, not that it was a race of course, but I coasted pass several canal boats. Old hand boaters were fully adapted to the slow pace of life, smiling and at ease, while new renters fresh from Trevor basin sometimes had panic in their eyes, oversteering this way and that, scanning the route ahead for any long boats in the narrow channel. Further away from the marina, they too were synchronising their rhythm with the surroundings and relaxing and laughing at what all the fuss was about. I imagined a single molecule of water flowing past me, which would go on to be processed through some distant treatment works

1. *The Hand of Industry*, 2. *Light Show to commemorate the ten-year anniversary of the WHS in 2019*

and gush out of a tap, in a quiet sunlit kitchen, into a kettle, somewhere in South Cheshire, having completed an incredible journey. The canal follows the contours of the valley, in tune with nature, a gravity fed tree lined wildlife corridor.

I took a break at Trevor, where a cool beer was just the ticket. A framed newspaper cutting on the wall of the Sun Inn showed the carnage of the Trevor Bank accident of 1945, when the canal wall collapsed, washing away a section of the Ruabon to Barmouth railway line which ran directly below, de-railing a train with the sad loss of the driver's life.

Llangollen Wharf sits pleasingly on a hill overlooking the bridge, where tourists are drawn like iron filings to a magnet. Once the supply and despatch point for the town, a derrick remains on the canal side. An atmospheric spot with colourful day stables for the horses who draw the boat trips to Horseshoe Falls, before they are walked back through the town to their home fields.

I decided to continue along the canal, to its end, to go with the flow (or against it) before exploring Llangollen town. Long strands of green weed waved and hypnotised me with their rhythmic nodding, willing me into a watery underworld, the ferns and their reflections appeared to grip the water surface, fish rose and kissed the surface, an eel skirted the edge of the weed and then was lost.

Nearing the source of the canal, it is drawn ever closer to the mother river which changes markedly in character, as the truly Alpine Dee clamours white and fizzes over and between huge grey rocks. The Robbers Leap, or Llam y Lleidr, is said to be in this area. Borrow was guided to the spot where a highly dangerous leap had been made across the rocks over a deep pool to escape pursuers. There was no such high drama rush to accompany my visit, it was far more tranquil, as the smell of exotic tobacco drifted up from a girl sat at the water's edge watching the Dee falling through the valley.

The first chain bridge was built in 1817 by Exuperius Pickering, of the docks at Trevor basin fame, who saw the potential in using the new canal to avoid paying the tolls which were charged to transport his coal, lime, and iron over Llangollen bridge. There have been several incarnations of the bridge since then on this wild stretch of river, a photo on a nearby interpretation board shows the Dee flooding through the tangled remains of one of them. The current bridge was thankfully restored in 2015, a walk across her in calmer times is a delight.

This area is a spaghetti junction of bridges, in addition to the pedestrian chain bridge, a short distance upstream stands the stone bridge connecting the roads on either side of the Dee, which goes beneath the bridge carrying the Llangollen railway. Parallel to this, Telford's A5 is in turn arched to let a tributary of the Dee flow below her, the whole interchange is a wonderful web of gracefully flowing lines and arches of brick and stone.

The horseshoe falls are an echo of the nearby and equally impressive horseshoe pass. The J-shaped weir was constructed by Telford to feed the canal, and as is usual with Telford's works, it is immensely pleasing on the eye. A short curtain of white water is formed which sweeps across the river, a giant oak is reflected in the mirror-calmed surface, a purple-flowered rhododendron dips over the weir, a heavy, brown-rusted chain secures a bleached rough- stripped tree trunk across the deflected flow, preventing surface debris entering the canal. If Disney did weirs, this could be their template.

The Chain bridge

The Holy Dee

The re-directed water flows through a Meter House where it is controlled and measured. An interpretation board informs that around 12 million gallons of water are drawn daily to feed the canals, and for drinking water. The need for a constant supply of water here required innovative hydraulic engineering works to be carried out some twenty-two miles upstream. The intrepid duo of William Jessop and Thomas Telford expanded Llyn Tegid (Bala Lake) into a reservoir by the addition of sluices so that the water level in the Dee did not drop too low in the summer months.

This is the highest point of the canals alongside the Dee, their story is a fascinating one, built for speed, and replaced by faster railways and roads, then resurrected for water supply and slow tourism.

Horseshoe Falls

9. Llangollen

"Life is sweet, brother ... There is night and day, brother, both sweet things; sun, moon and stars, brother, all sweet things; there is likewise the wind on the heath. Life is very sweet, brother; who would wish to die"? George Borrow.

The Afon Cyflymen, or fast flowing stream, falls from the Berwyn mountains through the suburbs on the south side of Llangollen. Its energy has been used to power mills to process corn and wool since before the 1800s. On the lower reaches of the stream, on a site behind Church Street, a flannel mill was supplanted by a tannery which operated from around 1900 until its closure in 1990. The Sun Brewery, a more pleasant-smelling enterprise, also operated in this area, its associated pub of the same name, remains, while the attractive Capel Pont Felin Hen, dating back to 1773, which it used as a warehouse after it ceased to function as a chapel, retains the aura of a spiritual house.

There were several other breweries in Llangollen, George Borrow even wrote a quatrain about its brown ale which was 'with malt and hop rife'. The Pen y Bryn Brewery on Berwyn Street operated from around 1840, later becoming known as Tanqueray's Llangollen Brewery and was the major brewery in the town until its closure in the 1930s.

Mills had operated in the Llangollen area since the arrival of the Cistercian monks at Valle Crucis, the industrial revolution led to larger scale operations, processing new materials. The Lower Dee Cotton Mills opened in 1805 just downstream of the bridge, a sluice gate and turbine runner remain in the quiet leafy riverside gardens. The mill was later re-purposed to take advantage of the prospering wool trade and operations expanded into the Upper Mill in 1855, which ceased production in the early 1920s, while the lower mill continued until the 1960s. Mile End Mill operated on the upstream side of the town from the 1870s and was affected by several fires.

George Borrow, having "become tired of the objects around us" in his East Anglia home "conceived that we should be all the better for changing the scene for a short period" and determined upon going into Wales, to pass a few months there. He was to make Llangollen his base, while his wife and daughter travelled here by train, he preferred to leave Chester on foot over the noble Dee Bridge "as by walking I should be better able to see the country ... than by making the journey with the flying vehicle". Borrow could eat miles on foot as easily as a hearty breakfast, he also consumed languages including Welsh which he had learned in Norfolk from books and a Welsh groom at the solicitors where he worked. In return for protection from torment for the groom for being a "Taffy" from his brother clerks, he received instructions in Welsh, especially pronunciation, for he was already stronger than the groom in book Welsh. The result of his energetic walks and enquiries was the classic book 'Wild Wales'.

A plaque on the wall of Dee Cottage on Mill Street commemorates his stay. Soon after arriving there he set the tone of his book when he wrote how 'a poor black cat entered and mewed piteously. It was skin and bone and had an eruptive malady and a bronchitic cough. It belonged to a local vicar and had been left behind at his departure. His successor brought with him dogs and cats, who, conceiving that the late vicar's cat had no business at the vicarage drove it forth to seek another home, which however it could not find. Almost all the people of the suburb were dissenters and knowing the cat to be a church cat, did all they could to make it miserable. Stone it, hang it, drown it! were the cries of almost everybody. Did instinct draw it towards us (as *fellow Anglicans*)? The good woman of the house was horrified, she saw the church cat on her carpet and made towards it, but the Borrows told her that they did not expect it to be disturbed, she let it alone, they fed it bread and butter and a little tea and sugar. It became their own cat, one of their family and through good treatment it soon lost its ailments and became sleek and bonny'.

Thomas Pennant described Llangollen as "a small and poor town... watered by the Dyfrdwy which runs with great passion through the valley... ancient castle Brân, is uncommonly grand. I know of no place in northern Wales where the refined lover of picturesque scenes can give a fuller indulgence to his inclination".

We had been to Llangollen many times

before, enjoying fine meals and those picturesque scenes, in fleeting visits compared to those of Borrow. We determined to get to know her better over the summer, and during those visits, the question which we kept asking ourselves was, why haven't we done this before?

Our first visit, in early July, was to the international eisteddfod, something we had been aware of for years, one of those things 'on the back burner'. On a warm Friday afternoon an appreciative, and interactive crowd were entertained in front of the war memorial by a series of performers, as a warm-up for the Parade of Nations which kicks off the party. A young Irish group clad in the green of the Emerald Isle charmed us with soft lilting songs and clog dances, the sound of which were amplified by metal discs placed on the ground. A choir of serene Finnish ladies were next, singing melodies of the north followed by a hugely energetic and theatrical performance by a Zimbabwean dance group. Three quite different performances, but the thing they had in common was the universal smiles on their faces. The parade was a snaking feast of colour and sound, beaming Punjabi dancers in full costume with fantailed headdresses, rustic Albanian pipe players, immaculate Canadian choirs, an ecstatic celebration of life.

The following day we were lucky enough to see the choir of the world competition, the pinnacle of the competitive sessions where the outright winner of the choral competitions is awarded the Pavarotti Trophy in memory of him and his father's long association with the festival. The range of acts on the stage was incredible, previously 'choir' for me was a bunch of people stood still belting out a song, but the innovation on display here was vast. There were highly choreographed displays, leaps and jumps, clapper-effects, dizzying on knees synchronisations, all in glorious technicolour. The winners were the National University Singapore Choir, as harmonious and smiling a group of young people as you could wish to meet. As we exited, a couple walking beside us remarked, "we can't believe we haven't done this before". The Llangollen International Eisteddfod is unique, one of the world's most inspirational cultural festivals, it drew us back again the following year when the main prize winners came from nearer to home with the excellent Johns' Boys of Rhosllannerchrugog, but the highlight for me was Catrin Finch, playing the harp to a modern keyboard accompaniment. I closed my eyes and allowed myself to be carried on the melodies up through the tiara roof of the pavilion and the slopes to the top of Dinas Brân and across to Valle Crucis Abbey and wondering if any harp playing as sweet as this, had been heard within their walls.

Another luxurious day brought us to the train station, where in the name of research, we had an excuse to dawdle, not that one is needed of course, but modern life just seems to encourage us to keep moving on, it is nice to weigh anchor now and again, or at least let out a storm drogue, and take it all in. The station is wonderfully atmospheric, well-travelled suitcases were piled on the platform where a round analogue clock awaits patiently for brief encounters. A steam train whistled its arrival onto the stage in its billowing cumulus clouds, passengers were guided off by waist-coated staff past old style ticket hatches, it was like being on the fringes of a theatre show. A few years ago, we were lucky enough to attend a wedding here, followed by a reception on the train, a truly wonderful day which will stay in my memory.

The bridge which has centre stage is traditionally thought to date back to 1345, though fragments of masonry found within the structure, have led some to suggest it may be later, it has since been modified to allow cars over her and trains beneath her. A castellated tower was removed from the northern end in 1940 to ease the flow of traffic, a great shame, I always enjoy a building on a bridge, no need for anything as extravagant as on the Ponte Vecchio, a simple tower would be plenty to keep me entertained. Widened and lengthened to accommodate the extra square interloper opening for the railway line, she remains a living structure, a focal point, a conveyor of goods and people, an old lady of the river.

When Dylan Thomas was sent to report on the eisteddfod of 1953, legend has it that he paid a boy to bring the results to him in a local bar, his description of "the white-horsed River Dee hisses and paws over the hills of its stones and under the greybeard bridge" confirms we are following in his footsteps and he could not resist the view from bridge. Of the town he wrote "When you leave the last voices and

measures of the sweet-throated, waltzing streets, the lilt and ripple of the Dee leaping, and the light of the night, to lie down, and the strewn town lies down to sleep in its hills and ring of echoes, you will remember that nobody was surprised at the turn the town took and the life it danced for one week of the long, little year". Pure magic.

There are convenient recesses on the cutwatered buttresses which slice the swelling Dee. White water rafters whooped and shrieked as they were buffeted by the rapids below us, tourists peered over excitedly as locals passed to stock up on groceries. Coracle fishing for salmon was a common sight here until the 1950s, just upstream at the Corn Mill, now a pub-restaurant a photo on the wall shows a salmon hung from a door frame, which extends from the shoulder to the calf of the three-piece suited gent standing next to it. A large water wheel is still in place at the mill which was founded by the monks of Valle Crucis Abbey. The present mill was re-built in 1786 and closed in 1974. We continued upstream along Victoria promenade where families enjoyed the warm sunshine on the flat rocks in a curve of the river on the edge of town. Richard Wilson painted the view downstream from here, giving Dinas Brân a lofty classical appearance. The bridge, corn mill and church tower, shown behind workers engaged in hard honest toil on the riverbank, are still recognisable today.

At St Collen's Church we admired the work and devotion in the pair of carved oak hammer-beam ceilings installed in 1450. The ancient wooden door by the font dates to the 12th century and may have come from Valle Crucis Abbey. Llangollen takes its name from this church which was

1. A view from Llangollen bridge, not your regular town centre view;
2. Time passes on the riverside path

founded in the sixth century by Saint Collen, a Christian warrior and later hermit who reputedly retired here after vanquishing a local man-eating giantess. A good enough reason as any to retire, others would follow him for altogether different reasons. In the churchyard we paused at the triangular monument to the Ladies of Llangollen, the runaway Irish aristocrats who set up home in Plas Newydd and turned into a gothic fantasy of stained glass and carved oak. Their "Romantic retirement" captured the imagination of Regency society as they welcomed many of the celebrities of the day including Sir Walter Scott and William Wordsworth, who penned a sonnet to the Ladies, who reportedly took umbrage to his description of Plas Newydd,

A stream to mingle with your favorite Dee
Along the Vale of Meditation flows ...
In ours the Vale of Friendship, let this spot
Be nam'd, where faithful to a low roof'd Cot

Lady Eleanor Charlotte Butler, is commemorated in the warmest of words... Late of Plas Newydd in this parish, deceased 2nd June 1829, aged Ninety Years, daughter of the Sixteenth, Sister of the Seventeenth Earls of Ormonde and Ossory... endeared to her many friends by an almost unequalled excellence of heart and by manners worthy of her illustrious birth the admiration and delight of a very numerous acquaintance from a brilliant vivacity of mind undiminished to the latest period of a prolonged existence...Sarah Ponsonby died soon after in 1831, not long surviving her beloved companion.

We heard a call from behind us "You can see them inside, near the cenotaph, there's a lovely marble plaque on the wall". Before we knew it, we were being whisked back into the church by a man with a carrier bag, who asked where are you from... where are you staying... are they looking after you? He switched the lights on and took us to the marble relief on the south wall, which puts faces to the names of the ladies. Our 'guide' kept calling me "Sir" I almost felt like George Borrow in 1854. As we bade farewell, we called out for him to enjoy his fish and chips, for we discovered once we were inside that he was on his way home in time to catch the news with his tea, and that when he saw us kindly went out of his way to share his knowledge of the church. A man coming into the Churchyard hearing our goodbyes smiled and said "Ah, you've met Gwyn then, heart of gold". Indeed, if every town had a Gwyn how sweet life would be.

On another visit to Llangollen, when I was treated to a tour by a local guide, I learnt that the monument may in fact not be a likeness of the ladies at all. It was installed by Mary Gordon a year after the release of her historical novel *Chase of the Wild Goose* in 1936, which was based on their lives. The ladies had died over 100 years prior to this and disliked having their portraits painted, so images of them are scarce, one theory is that one of the ladies is represented by the author and the other by the sculptress.

A few days later, we decided to go to Plas Newydd. We went without giving the visit much thought, almost as the completion of a kind of an un-written 'to do' list for Llangollen. Within seconds of arriving, we were completely bowled over. The black and white porched building, fronted by green ornamental trees in a zen-like gravel garden with Dinas Brân Castle and the grey limestone cliffs of Eglwyseg as a backdrop, under a blue sky, broken with soft white cauliflower clouds was perfect, no wonder they settled on this spot.

The house is unique, an adventure into 'gothicisation' as part of their 'oak carving mania'. Some fragments of the fine stained glass are thought to have come from Valle Crucis Abbey, the spoils of which were scattered far and wide. The grounds were a further unexpected delight, the circle of stones from the Gorsedd ceremony of the eisteddfod of 1908 form a magnetic

SARAH PONSONBY   ELEANOR BUTLER

The Ladies of Llangollen?

attraction on the lawned foreground which falls away to the Dell and Nant Cyflymen with its bower and font, also from the Abbey.

The ladies had been born into aristocratic families which gave them many privileges, but the consequent price was that they were expected to obey the social mores of that time, especially their family's expectations for their marriages. They found freedom here to live life how they wanted, carving out a 'life of sweet and delicious retirement'.

I was re-acquainted with Dinas Brân Castle when I joined a 'Castles and clifftops walk' as part of the Llangollen walking festival. On the ascent from the town centre, we were told that one of the walks in the festival included 'heart attack hill' I don't think this was it, but it came close.

Sections of the ramparts of an iron age hillfort can still be seen around the castle which was built by Prince Gruffudd ap Madoc around 1260. It had a short active life, being burnt in advance of Edward I's invasion, and abandoned soon after.

Brân is the Welsh word for crow, while cigfran refers to a raven, sculpted figures of which sit on top of the gateposts around the base of the castle, while the real thing can be seen at the top, black as a cow's belly. In the legend of Brân, he quarrelled with his twin brother Beli over the kingdom they had inherited and were about to go into battle when their mother Corwenna intervened. Peace was made, Brân built his fortress here, we shall learn more of Corwenna later.

Another legend tells the tale of a Norman knight, Payn Peverill, who wished to prove his courage by staying overnight in the castle, despite having been cautioned about the evil spirit of the giant Gogmagog who plagued the hilltop… the giant appeared, and a battle ensued, with Payn striking the fatal blow. With his final breath Gogmagog told of hidden treasures, including a golden ox, but failed to reveal their location.

I made a return visit to the castle to watch a sunset, slowing my ascent, to a snail-like conquering of the hill which allowed me to fully appreciate the views as they developed in front of me. I saw the silvery Dee snaking towards me from the east under the sunlit span of the A483 and the warm stone arches of the Cefn railway

Winter is coming at Dinas Brân

viaduct. A skylark rose above me singing his heart out, a buzzard hovered in the breeze at eye level, the dying sun lighting his undersides, his black head scanning the land below for his supper. The grey rolling wave of the Eglwyseg rocks cut obliquely across the landscape like a petrified Tsunami, snubbing its nose at the sky. The orange haloed hills to the west softened as the sun fell away, fern clad Velvet Hill was dabbed with bluebells giving her a hint of purple. An easy descent through the bat-shared twilight took me back to my campervan and waiting kettle.

I left Llangollen, driving along the high street early on a bright sunny morning,

and in my mind, completely verified what Borrow had been told of the Tylwyth Teg (Fairies) who existed hereabouts, for there in broad daylight, looking into a shop window were two fairies, with long locks of hair flowing over their lustrous winged dresses. When I looked back in my rear-view mirror, they had disappeared. In Welsh folklore, fairies are said to be friendly but mischievous, often living in caves and on mountains, maybe this was a trick, visible only to me? I have to say I was mildly disappointed to learn later that it was the weekend of the Llangollen Faery Festival and their beguiling artifice was not purely aimed at me.

Borrow had also been told a darker supernatural tale of a woman who had seen a 'corpse candle' proceeding from her cousin's house three nights before he died, prognosticating his death. This was similar to John Aubrey's historic account of a light appearing over the water when any Christian is drowned in the river "by which means they do find the body: and it is therefore called the Holy Dee".

At Valle Crucis Abbey I was lucky enough to be able to select a pitch at the camp site directly in front of the west wall. We have parked up our camper van in many fantastic locations over the years, all over the U.K., in France and Spain, but this is as scenic as any of them, and a much shorter drive from our home.

I last came to the abbey over 30 years ago, it was great to revisit, I particularly enjoyed the computer-generated day in the life of a monk which reminded me of how wild and isolated this spot would have been in 1201 when the Cistercian monks arrived here. The solitude of the valley would have suited the austere and agricultural lifestyles of the Cistercians. From the fishpond, the only remaining monastic fishpond in Wales, the ruinous remains of the abbey, stand bare against the backdrop of the hills. Moments of peace can still be found here, despite the busy campsite surroundings, I could almost hear the prayers of the white monks and see the lay monks toiling in the fields, it's easy to see why it appealed to the romantics, Turner painted the abbey in 1794.

In the former monk's dormitory, later to become the Abbot's Hall, a superb collection of sculptured grave slabs, some whole, others fragmentary which have been found within or near the abbey are laid out in roughly chronological order extending from the enigmatic stone staircase. Dating from 1290, the slabs are from the tombs of important local families who either founded or supported the various religious houses. As I took a quiet moment in there (a highly recommended pursuit) a shaft of sunlight caught a feather falling from a nest in the eaves, the chirping of sparrows and swallows echoed off the stone floor and walls.

The CADW produced guidebook details "This slab and the grave beneath it were found in front of the high altar of the church. Recovered in 1956, it is perhaps the finest surviving monument of this period in North Wales, with the carving almost in perfect condition... the inscription reads 'Here lies Madog son of Gruffudd called Fychan'... Madog ap Gruffudd (d.1306) was the great grandson of the founder of the abbey... he was the great-grandfather of Owain Glyn Dŵr. Indeed, Glyn Dŵr was able to claim that he was the sole surviving direct male descendant of one of the Welsh princely dynasties".

I walked away from the abbey to see if it was possible to reconstruct the composition of Turner's watercolour with Dinas Brân in the background. I suspected he had used poetic licence to align the two but was pleased to find his arrangement is accurate, though the abbey is understandably made prominent. His tree-veiled abbey and smoke issuing farmhouse is now much restored and cleansed, though the foreground is filled with the campsite, as opposed to the rustic scene of the pig wallowing pond attended by a young girl. Some views are best left to painters, I put my camera away, sat on the grass and took it all in.

I had a very peaceful night's sleep in the campervan. My sister camped in virtually the same spot on a visit with her daughter and had altogether a different experience when, it being a warm night, she decided to sleep outside the tent on a bale of straw and awoke in the early hours convinced she was been strangled by a medieval knight.

The abbey took its name from the Latin for valley of the cross, which in turn took its name from Eliseg's pillar, the ninth century cross erected by Concenn/Cyngen of Powys to commemorate his ancestors. A brief diversion took me up the valley to the remains of the pillar which sits in a glorious position in the middle of the valley, on top of a barrow mound which is

1 2 3

thought to be Bronze Age or Romano British and would have given the cross additional prominence. It was a blunt statement of royal authority to broadcast Powys' independence in defiance of English aggression from across the border. The interpretation board goes on, "Authority is claimed from the church and heaven above, but his heritage was plugged into a source of power from the land itself with deep roots both ancient and mysterious".

Pennant wrote: "I met with the remainder of a round column, perhaps the most ancient of any British inscribed pillar now existing. It was entire until the civil wars of the last century when it was thrown down and broken by some ignorant fanatics who thought it had too much the appearance of a cross to be suffered to stand. The pillar had been a sepulchral cross; folly and superstition paid it the usual honours".

A representation of the pillar can be seen in Llangollen Museum complete with the inscription which is denuded on the original.

1. *Valle Crucis Abbey; 2. The gravestone of Madog ap Gruffudd; 3. Eliseg's Pillar*

Returning to the river, just above Horseshoe Falls a sign at St. Tysilio Church announces, 'A place of pilgrimage – open every day', a warm welcome to a very peaceful place which enchanted me for several hours. I was drawn to the window with the image of St. James, patron saint of pilgrims, where I took out my key ring, and opened the worn metallic scallop shell, just to check he was still with me. 'The Cistercian Way' a modern pilgrim route connects here to Valle Crucis and goes on to include St. Winefride's Well and Basingwerk Abbey, the whole of the walk is some 650miles around the heart of Wales, a fantastic prospect... but not for today. In the designated living church yard, the grass is cut just twice a year to encourage wildflowers to flourish and birds to feed and nest. The gravestones tell their stories to the long listening yews, Exuperius Pickering our industrialist entrepreneur friend is tucked away near the entrance, where his monument bears the epitaph which he himself wrote.

I took a last look at the Horseshoe falls, to be hypnotised once more by the whispering arc of falling water. This spot was known for its beauty before Telford re-arranged the topography. Edward Pugh drew the scene in 1794, from which an engraving was made which was published in a set of 'Six views in Denbighshire'. Pugh was a Welsh-speaking artist and writer, the son of a Ruthin barber. His tour of north Wales, *Cambria Depicta* is the first by a writer whose first language was Welsh and is more sympathetic to the rural inhabitants and the condition of the poor than the travelling-gentry writers of the time. His view (reproduced on the cover) shows a young gentleman standing on a rock which is jutting out into the flow below a cascade of white water. He is holding aloft a fishing rod; others nearby are also fishing by rod or net.

To my untrained eye, it's a simple scene of young men engaged in fishing. John Barrell in his book on Pugh, delves much deeper. He notes how the young gentlemen is more elegantly dressed than the others and that he is elevated above them. He also notes that Llantisilio Hall is not shown, when a slight change of viewpoint would have allowed it to be included, as other artists had done before him. The title of the picture – "A Fall on the Dee, near the Vale of Crucis" refers to the abbey, located around a mile away, and not Llantisilio, the immediate location of the view. He explores the reasons for the "little of drama of inclusion and exclusion" played out in the engraving. Llantisilio Hall was the seat of Thomas Jones Esq. and, to depict it, convention would necessitate that it be included in the title, with the appropriate legend. Pugh probably realised that this was his best opportunity to inscribe one of his six views to the richest of all potential patrons, Sir Watkin Williams Wynn (the 5th Baronet) of Wynnstay whose recent coming of age had been lavishly celebrated. The Wynns had recently sold the abbey and lands adjoining it but remained the lords of the manor of Valle Crucis and the recipient of the tithes of the parish. Pugh chose to omit the hall and position the tiny church of Llantisilio at the centre of the picture, which he inscribed to Sir Watkin. John Barrell ponders if the young gentlemen standing bright and tall in the midst of the scene is Sir Watkin himself.

It seems that it wasn't enough just to be a skilled artist at that time, the arrangement of the 'simple scene' in the picture is the result of walking a compositional tightrope to give the best possible chance of future patronage.

Llantysilio west window. The plaque below commemorates the poet Robert Browning reading the lesson here. He was a visitor to nearby Bryntysilio.

Saint Tysilio

10. In the shadow of the Berwyn

At Glyndyfrdwy, Sophia joined me, we crossed the grey stone bridge and walked past the volunteer manned railway crossing into the village. At the top of the hill a novel use has been found for the old red telephone box as an information centre. There are leaflets about the area, numerous books and intriguingly a boxed set of 'desperate housewives' DVD's.

A short distance up the valley stands Owain Glyndŵr's mount. A stile with the logos of Cadw and the Welsh Assembly (Senedd) now gives access to a permissive path over private land to this historic feature. The way leads up to the fir and oak topped summit where an interpretation board informs "It was here on 16th September 1400 in front of 300 of his followers, that Owain Glyndŵr was proclaimed or proclaimed himself Prince of Wales. This defiant act triggered a war against English rule lasting six years. Glyndyfrdwy was Glyndŵr's home turf – away from prying eyes of sheriffs or English nobles; somewhere to rally his supporters. His hall was probably a timber-framed building sited in the field below the mound. It was razed to the ground by the English in 1403".

Glyndŵr was known for his support of poets and bards, he was educated in law, well read, a soldier, a diplomat, and a courtier to Richard ll. The rebellion was triggered when, following the accession of Henry IV, Lord Gray of Ruthin seized a tract of land to which Glyndŵr laid claim, he took the matter to court but was discredited. When the Bishop of St. Asaph warned that if redress was not found, danger was imminent, some of the lords replied that "they did not fear that rascally bare footed people".

As a descendant of the ancient princes of Powys, the rulers of Deheubarth and the royal house of Gwynedd, Glyndŵr had a fine pedigree to be proclaimed as the rightful native Prince of Wales. He was the son of prophecies going back to Merlyn, who foretold that Britain would be reclaimed by the Britons, frequent unsuccessful attempts were made to subdue him leading to him achieving a mystical status. Shakespeare had Henry IV describe him as 'that great magician, damn'd Glendower' and in the play Glyndŵr himself is given the following words 'I say the earth did shake when I was born/ The heavens were all on fire, the earth did tremble/ I can call spirits from the vasty deep'. Several of Henry IV's attacks on Wales were thwarted by foul weather, as we saw near Bangor on Dee, Welsh forces would appear and disappear in the mist of the hills, the revolt gathered momentum across Wales.

He held parliaments in Machynlleth and Harlech attended by men from each part of Wales and laid the foundations for an independent Welsh Church and universities. In 1405 he would sign the 'Tripartite Indenture' with Henry Percy (The Earl of Northumberland) and Edmund Mortimer (his son-in-law). Under the treaty, England and Wales would have been divided into three parts ruled by Percy, Mortimer and Glyndŵr who would rule Wales and the western counties of England including the whole of Cheshire. Glyndŵr's share is some measure of his standing at this stage. He was bolstered by French support and having Edmund Mortimer by his side gave him substantial bargaining power. This, however, would be the height of his success, Henry IV, who had usurped the English crown lower down the Dee at Flint, was initially in a weak possession with threats on many fronts. Gradually, he would consolidate his position, quelling rival claims to the throne and resolving dangers from Scotland and France. He secured more money from the treasury to fund his campaigns, regaining control of the lands from Glyndŵr.

French support came to an end, Aberystwyth Castle was lost in 1407 and Harlech two years later. 1409 saw the death in battle of Edmund Mortimer and the capture of Owain's wife, two of his daughters and three grandchildren, all of whom were to die in the Tower of London. In the latter years of the rebellion, Owain and his followers were fighting a guerrilla war, he went into hiding, possibly in the Berwyn mountains just to the south of here. He ignored all offers of pardon and is thought to have died around 1415, conceivably while being sheltered in a sympathetic household in the marches. He was never betrayed by his countrymen, despite the desolation and hardship which followed more than a decade of civil war and the large rewards offered for his head. Wales now has an independent church and

Senedd (Parliament), in 2008 the North East Wales Institute for further education in Wrexham became Glyndŵr University, his spirit lives on.

Just before Carrog, we came across a footpath along the north bank, the first for a while, and what a treat it is. As we walked down from the road, Sophia saw a kingfisher fly up from the opposite bank, a short distance later a cormorant took off noisily as his wings slapped the water surface. It is a lovely quiet spot, gnarled and twisted hawthorns and hazel trees lined the bank, chunky isolated stone islands provided landing stages for dippers. We heard the first steam train of the day approaching from Llangollen, glimpsing her through gaps in the trees as she neared Carrog station, clouds of white steam flowed past her happy faced carriages. We sat for un-measured time, just listening to the soft lapping of water on stone.

The search for Mabon ap Modron
The Grey Owl of Cawlwyd brought them to the Eagle of Gwernabwy (near Carrog*) who told them he had not heard of Mabon, but would be their guide to a Salmon with whom he had made peace on his travels, and he knew of no one else more ancient or wise...
(** See earlier note re the Mabinogion*)

Our pitch at Carrog Station campsite was on raised ground next to the river, which was visible through a gap in a hedge of early fruiting apple and blackthorn trees, a kingfisher, dipper, and several herons passed us by. We walked along the river in front of the village where houses are built high and cling to the steep sided bank in Positano style, vying for the best spot in the sun. Picnickers, stone skimmers and paddlers enjoyed the easy days of summer.

The bridge is probably my favourite on the Dee, five-arched in strong grey stone, the buttresses have recesses for pedestrians to avoid the traffic of the single carriageway which she carries, two of them have benches, an invitation to sit and linger too good to be missed. A nearby stone is dated 1661, I wondered how many people have sat and rested here, watching the business of the valley taking place in the rhythm of the day and the seasons.

1. Glyndŵr's Mount; 2. Carrog Bridge; 3. The Grouse and the bridge at Carrog. Perfect harmony.

Exploring a quiet corner of the village, I found a stone pillar which marks the site of Glyndŵr's prison house which stood until the late 20th century. A black and white photo pinned to the fence shows the thick stone walls beneath a dilapidated slate roof.

The original twelfth century church of Llansantffraid (St. Bridget) also stood nearby until it was washed away by floods in 1601. The new church, located safely high up in the village was built in 1612. Until the coming of the railway, the village was known as Llansantffraid Glyndyfrdwy.

I crossed the final section of the Afon Morwynion before she joins the Dee, she set me a puzzle a few years ago when I followed a tributary of the river Alun to a wooded area beneath Cyrn-y-Brain where the watersheds of both fledging rivers are connected by a drainage ditch, shown on the map as a blue line, the flow from the north side of the trees goes into the Alun, while the flow from the south side goes into the Morwynion to arrive at this confluence. The tributary waters from the woods of the two neighbouring watersheds will meet again just downstream of Holt.

From the Grouse Inn we had a widescreen view over the bridge and river to the history-scarred hills on the opposite side of the valley where the spoil of a slate mine spilled onto purple-grey terraces. An oblique line of trees marks the incline which would have transported the hard-earned contents of the hill to the valley floor.

I awoke in the early hours and sat outside the van to see a pristine star-spangled sky across which four shooting stars flashed in the following half hour. Now and again, the silence was broken by the rumble of a truck heading along Telford's A5 to catch the ferry from Holyhead. Even the tawny owl we had heard earlier was now silent.

As I walked along the river at 5am, I wondered if I had adopted the pattern of the Cistercian monks of Valle Crucis Abbey; I was early to bed last night, up at 2am for starry Matins and here I was worshipping nature in Lauds. I shared the path with swallows and bats, to a curve in the river where I sat under a shattered oak. A buzzard flew silently over me, a white orb traveling low near the opposite bank materialised into a dipper, a heron flew directly at me, apparently not noticing my honouring of the noetic dawn, then at the last minute he swerved away, flustered that his fishing peg was occupied.

I returned to the quietly stirring campsite from where we walked to the adjacent and atmospheric Carrog station, an original from 1865 which is lovingly preserved. We boarded the train which took us along the line to Corwen which hugs the Dee, where we saw fly-lines glinting and whipping in the sun above wadered anglers. From the station we walked through the community orchard, past the spot where 'The Pavilion' once stood, an entertainment venue which Ken Dodd described as 'the best tin shed he had ever appeared in'. Erected just before the First World War it is said to have been a recycled tram shed from Birkenhead which was later extended to enable up to 4,000 people to attend many varied events including the first Urdd national eisteddfod and speeches by Lloyd George and Aneurin Bevan. It also hosted concerts, sheep-shearing contests, cultural and sporting activities, sadly, costly structural faults brought almost a century of loyal service to an end when it was demolished in 2015.

In the square there is a fine statue of Owain Glyndŵr on horseback with sword held aloft. I was puzzled. Jim Perrin had described it as 'comic-grotesque – a fork-bearded, wellington-booted, malignant, ill-proportioned and supplicant dwarf'. I did a bit of research and found that this statue replaced the original in 2007, after Perrins visit. I came across a photo of the original and all became clear. We heard the soft Welsh spoken, true to Taliesin's prophecy amid the clatter of flat-bed lorries, stacked high with bristling tree trunks. Corwen is perched above a fertile crook of the Dee and has long been a major crossroads in North Wales, sitting on the London to Holyhead as well as the historic Bala to Chester routes.

The name Corwen is said to derive from 'The white choir' or from Queen Corwenna, the mother of Brân of Castell Dinas Brân fame. Interpretation boards in the market square give a vivid account of Corwen's history, from Caer Drewyn, the Celtic hillfort and the small Roman settlement where the town stands today, through Glyndŵr's revolt, to its importance as a stopping point for drovers and stage-coaches on Telford's A5. It is a place of agricultural fairs and markets and has often been a place of dissent, a quote from Highways and byways in North Wales by Arthur Bradley in 1898 is retold "the tone of the place is genuine and of the soil... it speaks unmistakably of generations of farmers dealing and chaffering, drinking and voting, and fighting in the streets."

The Owain Glyndŵr Hotel announces itself as "a coaching inn built c1740 with parts dating back to the 14th century. The first public Eisteddfod held here in 1789 set the pattern for today's eisteddfodau". That first eisteddfod was not without controversy, Gwallter Mechain, the winning poet, had been tipped off as to the theme of the required poem prior to the day of the competition, to the disadvantage of the other poets, a repeat of the skulduggery at another eisteddfod soon after at Bala, led to threats of a duel before a resolution was found. The town trail leaflet mentions the hotel was originally a monastery set in the grounds of the church which still stands to the rear. George Borrow, 'feeling rather thirsty' stopped here for about an hour 'refreshing myself' on his walk from Llangollen to Cerrigydrudion.

We had the pleasure of overnighting at the hotel when we attended the Corwen walking festival, also refreshing ourselves as we dined with a view over the graveyard before continuing our up-beat theme by joining an atmospheric ghost tour around the town as the light faded. The bat-skied rear of the manor house was particularly eerie as we learned of the grim conditions in there, and that the building behind us was in fact its morgue and the unmarked mound in the corner of the graveyard was the resting place of numerous children who passed away during their confinement. A fellow ghost walker asked about the 'Orissor College', which I had previously not heard of, but Chris our local font of knowledge was conversant. Frank Serpico, the brave corruption exposer within the NYPD, played by Al Pacino in the film of the events (in which he was shot and left un-aided by his colleagues in what is thought to have been a set-up), lived here in 1979 and 1980. In an interview with the Daily Post, he talked of how he got involved with a spiritualist group which he later described as 'cult-like' which ran courses at the manor house in natural healing, the mind, the environment, and self-reliance skills. He sank, and lost, all his money in the venture, but still speaks fondly of his time in Corwen. 'I liked the area's purity. I loved the trees' he says and has 'always longed to go back". Continuing our walk through a tea light illuminated courtyard we learnt of the ghosts of Roman soldiers who have been seen walking along the road; only their top halves being visible, as the level of the road was raised when Telford constructed the A5.

The view from Pen y Pigyn

The view from Pen y Pigyn is well worth the steep walk up from the town for the panorama over the broad sweep of the Dee through which extends around the town. The church is at the centre of it all, a circle within the arc. Caer Drewyn, on the opposite side of the valley is the southernmost in the line of iron age hillforts which run along the Clwydian range and is necklaced with a ring of stone. The old drover's path, Moel Famau with her Jubilee tower remnants, Llantysilio mountain and the Horseshoe Pass are laid out in a visual treat. To the east the silver snaking Dee wends her way to thrill holidaymakers at Llangollen.

Earlier, I had stood once more in front of Corwen Manor, although washed in warm daylight, it was still a cold prospect. Built in 1834 as a workhouse for 150 poor people, the grounds were separated into four yards where able-bodied residents worked for their keep. From my elevated viewpoint the cruciform shape was clearly visible, it is the only such workhouse left in Wales. It closed in 1940, which seems uncomfortably recent. Across the road from it once stood the Tramps Rest where vagrants could earn food and lodging by breaking a hundredweight of stone a day. I could see orange coveralled volunteers nearby working on the extension of the railway line, a noble task in a town familiar with hard work.

My walk back down to the town was painful on the knees, but pleasurable on the senses; stone walls and boulders were covered with luxuriant green mosses and lichens, fallen down trees lay amongst heather and bracken, dewy spiders' webs glistened in the sun as they caught falling pine needles.

Later at the museum I was met with a hearty 'good afternoon' and guided to the new exhibitions of the history of the Pavilion and the eisteddfod chairs. I also enjoyed the funky video of schoolchildren ascending Pen y Pigyn and from the top of which they collectively pointed their lightning sparking swords to the sky. On a previous visit I had seen the comprehensive timeline of the life of Owain Glyndŵr, while on the first floor there is a history of the railway at Corwen, from its arrival in 1865, its effect on the town and its departure in 1964 to its welcome return in 2015.

The church is accessed through the lych gate, immediately to the left of which are the 'kneeling stones' with recesses cut for the knees. Found only in this part of wales, it is thought they were used by widows to pray for their departed husbands.

The Church was founded in the sixth century by Breton-Welsh saints St. Mael and St. Sulien. This fact triggered a very pleasant memory of our 'Grand Tour' in our lovely old camper van the previous year which had started in the beautiful walled city of St. Malo in Brittany. I dug out my journal, where the notes I took on a guided tour (I can't help it) refer to St.

Malo being founded by Aaron, a 6th century Welsh-hermit monk who was followed by another Welshman, St. Maclou from where the name St. Malo is derived. Many Celtic Britons fled the instability in the centuries after the Romans withdrew, founding monastic settlements in what is now modern-day Brittany. The cordial modern-day Welsh-Breton relationship was cemented after the tour, with a bowl of moules mariniere washed down with fresh foamy beer.

The entrance porch has a curved and pointed pre-historic standing stone built into it, rising like a flame from the ground. The circular site in which the church sits is reminiscent of early sites of Christian worship. On our second visit here, which was a much brighter day than under the previous slate-grey sky, the stone appeared totally different, jutting much further out of the wall.

To the rear stands the base of an ancient preaching cross, resembling that at Eliseg, the only similar structure in the area. The lintel above the priest's doorway is carved with a cross which is said to be

Kneeling stones

the mark of Owain Glyndŵr's dagger which he threw from Pen y Pigyn hillside in a rage. If my land had been seized, and my family locked away in the tower of London, I would have probably been a little miffed too. The present building dates from the 1200s and is peaceful and welcoming. Behind the red-lined doors, an 11th century font sits below a dark wood-carved ceiling.

In the falling sun of early evening, I walked out from the centre, along a footpath past the football field and its clubhouse raised on breeze block stilts, a visible reminder of the flood plain meadow which local literature, and memory, tells is still prone to flooding and is the reason why the town lies snug on the lower slopes of its protective hill. A slate and shale tombstone fenced way led to a warmed riverine amphitheatre which I had all to myself. A curve of the river was split by an island, the lower parts of trees, were leaf bare and mud coated, holding up wattles of debris. A leaflet which I had picked up in the town mentioned the water's edge is home to otter and water vole, while the Dee is also renowned for salmon, brown trout and their beautiful relative, the grayling, sometimes called the 'lady of the streams' which prefer swift, clean running water, with deep currents and gravel beds, which is reflected in this area's name of Gro Isa. In the hour or so which I sat there in my camouflaged t-shirt, I must have almost become part of the riverbank, a pheasant strutted up almost close enough to touch, while passing geese barely noticed me. The local fly population were not so easily duped, circling in what seemed to me like the eager anticipation of my decomposition. As it was, the hope I had of seeing a water vole was not to be fulfilled, but an hour on the river is always a treat. A nearby notice with a faded print showed that Turner set up his easel around here, I am always happy to follow in his footsteps.

I left Corwen via the road bridge to the north, downstream the tree-covered stone abutments of the old Denbigh, Ruthin and Corwen railway lay almost parallel, a stone pillar stood in the middle of the flow, awaiting its Simeon.

A minor road leads up from near the bridge end to Caer Drewyn where I celebrated the sunset of the summer solstice soaking up the last warmth from the rays of the sun. A bird of prey, possibly a kite, came into sight very briefly and was gone, carried on the wind. The flat land of Dyffryn Edeirnion was already in shade, a fertile 'D' extending from the base of the Berwyn range, hemmed in by the Dee, which bides its time in reclaiming her. In the distance I could see the brooding peaks of the Arenig's, the source of our watery distraction. I imagined Owain Gwynedd gathering his men here before going on to engage with Henry II's huge army at Crogen. Sitting down near the cairn at the top, skylarks sang and tumbled and fell out of the sky, one landed on a fencepost just beneath me, less colourful than its song. The sun dipped behind a layer of grey cloud which veneered the horizon and deprived me of a blazing sunset photo opportunity, the views, the peace, and the space, more than made up for it. The sky darkened over the bowl of the fort, stars emerged as the twilight slipped from civil into nautical, all was quietening. Lights came on at Corwen, an alpine village below the bald peaks of the Berwyn, the lower slopes of which hold the town in steadfast embrace. I imagined people making final preparations for the night, locking in livestock from wolves as the year turned.

Joining the Clwydian Way, the path dropped down through thick towering bracken, to reach the tree-lined bank, through a gap in which I saw a flash of silver as a fisherman played in and swiftly released his catch. Swallows dipped and rose and twisted above, summer flies providing a bonanza for creatures above and below the water.

Nearing the grey-stone Pont Corwen, which has four central large arches and several smaller ones at the flanks, I could see rider-less bikes and canoes zoom past above the parapet, interspersed by caravans and lorries. A row of vertical stones ran parallel to the riverbank, like a long thin graveyard, curving away to where the bridge structure first rises from the ground, seemingly placed to guide flood waters away from surrounding fields. The Dee would seem to have been non-compliant over the years, some stones having been toppled over and one section of the bank had been washed away completely by a river meander.

The traffic which the bridge carries has increased many-fold over the years. There being no pavement, I looked in the direction of the Rhug estate, and could see pulses of traffic coming through the lights, I timed my pedestrian crossing accordingly, sadly only being able to catch glimpses of the expansive views from mid-bridge, for fear of my ungainly 'sprint' being curtailed by me being splattered like a fly on a windscreen.

I returned to the town centre before leaving with Sophia via a gorgeous tree lined path running above the A5. The traffic noise soon fell away as we connected with the sanctuary of the North Berwyn Way which follows the disused Ruabon-Barmouth railway line. A short distance along the path it appeared that we had wandered into someone's lovingly landscaped garden, a few steps later a GWR boundary marker confirmed we were indeed on the right track (or former track).

Between gaps in the trees, we saw fishermen flicking flies into promising areas of the waterflow, the lines glinting like spiders' webs caught on the breeze. We arrived at a cabin made of old railway sleepers, outside of which a stout bench invited us to take a rest. Inside the cabin,

1. Corwen Bridge; 2. Great Western Railway marker

birds' nests had fallen down the chimney in a jumble of twigs into the disused fireplace, while a starling's nest remained tucked between a beam and the roof. I wondered of the tasks that would have been done here at this spot which is now only accessible on foot. Within the building an interpretation board gave an unexpected but appreciated, overview of Freshwater Pearl Mussels, the existence of which I had previously been unaware of in the Dee. It informed of how they are one of the longest-lived invertebrates in Britain and grow to 14cm long, needing cool, clear, well oxygenated unpolluted water to survive. They have been exploited in Britain since pre-Roman times for the small dark coloured pearls that occasionally occur in them. Many people worked in the pearl industry in the nineteenth century, but it was not sustainable, the UK mussel population crashed, they became virtually extinct in many areas of England and wales. Living to more than 70 years old, they have not reproduced naturally on the Dee for more than 30 years; the remaining survivors are gradually dying of old age. An initiative is now underway which will hopefully secure their long-term survival.

The beautiful Church of Llangar crept up on us, sat behind a wall on a hill dotted with old farmhouses, from which smoke rose in a time stalled view. The door being closed, we took advantage of the idyllic setting above the confluence of the river Alwen with the Dee and sat on a bench at the top of the steeply sloping churchyard where the tombstones nod and tilt to the flowing waters below. According to legend, the church was to have been built near where the Cynwyd bridge crosses the river, but however hard the masons and builders worked to lay the stones during the day, they were mysteriously removed during the night. The counsel of a local wise man was sought, who told them to hunt for the white stag (Carw Gwyn) and wherever they first saw it, to build the church there. Fortuitous indeed how Llan Garw Gwyn, the Church of the White Stag, as it was originally named, came to be in this spot, another auspicious meeting of rivers. The exterior is brightly whitewashed, as most local churches were until Victorian times. Its present neat appearance, and indeed its survival, is due to a rescue operation by CADW, after over a century of abandonment and decay.

Sometime later, we took part in a 'Church and Chapel Walk' at the Corwen festival, which started at Corwen Church, then brought us here and finished off at Rhug chapel. A numinous golden triangle of a walk, for which Llangar church was opened. Inside is a real treat, from stone floor to timber roof, if I could borrow some of the words from the 'Enjoy Medieval Denbighshire' booklet produced by the councils tourism department "CADW's painstaking restoration... retained the towering three-decker pulpit; the box pews for gentry and rough benches for lesser mortals; and the singing gallery with its four-sided music stand...

No fewer than eight layers of wall paintings were rediscovered and restored, ranging from medieval saints and deadly sins within painted timber framing to the grim 18th century figure of death with dart, hourglass and gravediggers' tools. Here are five centuries of history, revealed without disturbing the powerful atmosphere of this lonely and magical place". This must be one of our favourite places on the Dee, a place of calm and peace, in a setting which befits a magical deer.

Rhug Chapel, the final site on our golden triangle walk, another moving beautiful building, deserves a further mention. J.S. Howson described how the 'quaint old chapel of Rug, is worth not only a visit, but almost a pilgrimage'. I will quote the booklet once more to give a taste of its delights "This gem of a building strikingly preserves the spirit of late medieval church decoration, exuberantly demonstrating what local painters and carpenters could do when given free rein by a wealthy patron who scorned puritan simplicity". Also, in the care of CADW, an exhibition details its colourful history as well as the restoration of Llangar from being propped up to prevent collapse, to the majestic building that exists today.

We left the railway path to follow a meander to where the Alwen, a major tributary, joins the Dee. Large stones have been arranged around the confluence to stabilise the banks. A sparrow hawk and a heron passed us in quick succession, followed by a Kingfisher which treated us to a fantastic display, flying electric blue along the centreline of the river, then banking in front of us showing her chestnut brown undersides, before peeping her way downstream. The path crosses back over the railway line and rises through a deliciously tree-lined hollow to the village of Cynwyd, where we obtained sustenance at the village shop. Pont Dyfrdwy also uses bulky stones, placed on the upstream side to protect her pillars from the floodwaters which sometimes come bounding down here from Bala, as we walked across, a couple paddled out slowly from the bank, careful footsteps seemingly placed through the experience of years.

On the roadside approaching Hendŵr, a chambered cairn, although initially not obvious amongst the undergrowth and soil, is substantial, with a massive top stone of at least 12 feet by 8 feet. The uprights are only partly visible, electric

supply lines run above the melancholy megalith.

After Cynwyd, the map once more shows no footpaths which follow the banks. The Dee here however sits under, and is fed by the beautiful Berwyn mountains, new territory to me and once again, the walking

1. *Llangar church sits above the confluence of the Alwen with the Dee;*
2. *Llangar church interior*

festival delivered a great opportunity.

From Hendŵr we walked up a steep, erratic, and oak-lined lane, in what seemed to be a skyward direction from the valley floor. My heart pumped at a rate not reached for many years, sweat formed on my brow, I could taste salt on my lips. We emerged from the trees at a crossroads of rough tracks, one of which curved upward around the base of the hill, from which sheep scattered, as we arrived at the striking stone circle of Moel Tŷ Uchaf. I circled the feature many times, pausing at what appears to be a heel stone to get the best possible photo, though a grey sky was not the ideal backdrop. There are several gaps in the stones which otherwise stand shoulder to shoulder. A magical spot, the distant Dee showed itself as a delicate silver ribbon meandering under a wooded bluff, towards Bala. Layers of hills and wide-open spaces stretched into the distance, I wondered if on quiet evenings Tylwyth Teg might dance up here.

A year later, an archaeological themed walk would take me back to the stone circle, after a hard, wet-backed, heart-pumping, calf-muscles-like-cheese-wire, slog up to and along, a windswept Berwyn Ridge. We had more time to view the 41 stones, in their big-small alternating arrangement which may signify use as a calendar, and to learn of the alignments which have been observed between some of the stones and a nick in the profile of the ridge on winter sunsets and summer sunrises.

The Holy Dee

As we squelched our way down, (it was more fun than it sounds) a fellow walker pointed out some cranberries. I was familiar with bilberries (Llys) but was not aware of any other berries growing on the heather moors. The co-walker was a botanist who kindly went on to show me three further types of berries, namely cowberry, crowberry and the fantastically named cloud berry, of which the fruits are like raspberries and are on their southern geographical limit here.

After the first visit, I did a quick online search for the stones, expecting to see photos of radiant sunrises, and the triumphant smiling faces of those who had managed to haul themselves up there in time to see it in compliant weather conditions. The search results drew me off on a complete and highly unexpected tangent. There were numerous accounts of how, on January 23rd, 1974, people in the villages of Llandderfel and Llandrillo reported hearing a huge bang, felt an earth tremor and saw brilliant lights in the sky above the Berwyn Mountains. As some ran from their homes, fearing another tremor, they saw a blaze of light on the mountainside. The Police received hundreds of calls and eyewitness accounts of the strange event, with reports of an object on the hillside, of lights, bright red, orange, white yellow and green, a large fire, an object with a tail travelling west. Some were convinced they had seen a UFO.

The Daily Post reported in 2019 that a new document had emerged which showed that a military exercise was taking place on the night and advising the coastguards that at least 10 aircraft were taking part and to expect at least 80 flashes around the Liverpool Bay area and North Wales coastline. I thought that this would clear up the story, although a UFO researcher was quoted as saying that he believed the operation was to flush UFOs out of the sea. But the article went on to say that in 2010, a key witness, a retired nurse, insisted that she saw something strange on the mountainside. After hearing a large bang and thinking it was a plane crash, she went to the scene to see if she could help. At the time she said: "It (the object) couldn't have got there any other way apart from being flown there, so it had to be a UFO of some sort. I'm talking about something that could only

Moel Tŷ Uchaf stone circle

have got there by flying and landing...the object glowed orange, red and yellow and was moon-like, but without windows or doors... I've never seen anything like it before or since. I have no idea what it was".

This was clearly an unusual event, witnessed by many and recorded with a magnitude of 3.5 on the Richter scale, the coincidence of the earth tremor with aerial lights seems unlikely, but is apparently not without precedent. The eyewitness accounts however add another dimension to the events, if there is intelligent life out there, looking for a new home, this would certainly make a very logical area to settle.

The Ceidiog falls blissfully through Llandrillo towards the Dee. On her banks, the spirit of George Borrow, the Romany Rye or Gypsy gentleman, shone upon me once more, when I came across five glorious Vardos, resplendent in green, red and yellow. The horses had been washed in the river and were being fed and watered, a stew was being prepared. Tasks for the evening revolved around Jack Evans, continuing a lifetime of travel into his 80th year. The talk around the fire was of places been, and yet to arrive at, of horse fairs at Appleby and Ballinasloe, the open road. This was an up-lifting experience, I can think of no better way of spending a few hours, long may the freedom of this simple way of life continue, in tune with the seasons and the landscape.

The rain fell gently as I arrived at Tyfos stone circle which is located on the other side of the valley, opposite to Moel Tŷ Uchaf. Seeing no access, I viewed them from the road. A small bank surrounds the circle of 15 stones which had far greater length than height, giving them the appearance of having fallen asleep or having been knocked over like dominos. Thought to date to the Bronze Age, another desecrating utility line runs above them, I am beginning to think that ley lines may have been tapped into as a new power source.

A footpath took me from Tyfos upstream to Cilan where the route of the old railway line and the Dee intersect once more, bedfellows who can never seem to leave each other on valley floor. I saw the unmistakeable forked tail of a red kite at the top of an old oak tree, it flew away flashing red and brown. The rain came down heavier, I put up my umbrella, in what my inner eye told me was Nicholas Crane on an epic long walk fashion, but as a squall buffeted me, I hoped no one could see me as I wrestled with it to prevent a Mary Poppins style incident.

I reached the double arched, grey stoned Cilan bridge in a soft mist. Stones protruded out of its walls in ugly house style, it was easy on the eye, despite being closed for repairs. The walkways on its flanks, supported by diagonal metal stays, were useful in providing shelter when I was hit by another feisty squall, tarps and signage for the ongoing work did not make for a good photo, but the car free road did however allow me to waltz down the middle of the carriageway in carefree safety, which was very satisfying.

The mist and low cloud partially cleared to reveal a deep blue sky, under which a small brilliant white cottage sat on a hill in a sea of radiant green trees. I walked up a wooded hill, behind an old farmhouse, where inquisitive horses cantered over to say hello, I heard the sharp call of a kingfisher close by on the river which was sadly hidden from me by the trees which lined the bank. Swallows cut across the sky making the most of the ample supply of insects before return south, rowan berries glistened in the still strong sun, but a fresh wall of saturated

The old ways

cloud obliterated all, and reminded me that summer was fading. The path emerges on the Llandderfel road, a back route to Bala which is much quieter than the A494. Lonely stone plinths sat on the roadside dreaming of milk churns, several pick-ups passed me, with bouncing salivating sheep dogs in the back, on their way to a trial near Llandderfel which I would later pass, a celebration of the countryside.

Just before Denbighshire becomes Conwy, another chambered cairn on the north bank was very atmospheric in the continuing mist, the cairn shared a raised mound with an oak and two hawthorns and a multitude of pheasants. The top stone is no longer visible, either reduced by the forces of attrition over time or possibly re-purposed, easing the burden on the vertical sides. I sat and paused for a while contemplating the cairns and stone circles of the valley, wondering how many others there would have been a thousand years ago.

Nearing Llandderfel a path led from the road, down a slope through trees, across which a squirrel carried an acorn. The first few oak leaves were turning red brown. An outfall at the base of the hill was choked with sweet-smelling, bee-buzzing invasive Himalayan Balsam. Walking across a lovely stretch of flood plain, I saw arches and openings in stonework on the opposite bank under which no water flowed, overflow routes preceding the long and beautiful 'Pont fawr' proper which sat below wispy cloud, quietly crossing, and prepared for the sometimes-tempestuous Dee.

In the village the houses hung pleasingly on the side of the misty hill, along streets which followed the wavy contour lines. Buddhist prayer flags blessed the footsteps between a house and its hill ascending outbuilding. It was late afternoon, there are no shops or inns, though the name plates on heavy stone lintels often identify the previous incarnations of the houses.

A stream ran through the centre of the village, past a new looking building which had a light outside that, in the falling dusk, drew me towards it like a moth. It was a village hall which a man and a lady, back-bone members of our rural communities, were waiting to close after a show, patiently waiting for a pot plant to be collected. They were proud of their new hall, as we chatted, he went inside to fetch an aerial photo of the previous one which had given many years of good service before being replaced. He pointed out various buildings and gave a short history of the village, of how the house next to the hall was one of several tanneries, the two cobblers, tailors, and a very much missed butcher. He was a mine of knowledge on the local area and confirmed my thoughts that despite it being a very dry summer, the Dee had a higher than expected water level which was being maintained for downstream extraction. He mentioned that despite the recent rain, the level in Llyn Celyn was very low and that some of the remains which had been flooded could be seen, the following morning I made a side trip, while the conditions were right... more on this later.

I mentioned Moel Tŷ Uchaf standing stones and the story I had come across about the events of 1974. The lady remembered as a small child sitting on the floor of their house and feeling the earth tremor which occurred that evening. The family went out but saw nothing, but others in the village saw much more when they went up the mountain to offer help at what they thought was an accident site. When I settled into my camper van for the night, at the base of the Berwyn mountains, I recalled the events and conversations of the day... and made sure that all the door catches were in the locked position. The late-night activation of the hazard lights on a nearby vehicle did nothing to aid my sleep.

I returned on a warm summer's day to visit St. Derfel's church which is dedicated to Derfel Gadarn, a warrior saint of the sixth century. On seeing the pulled-to door, I read a notice advising a key was available nearby, this wasn't necessary, the church was open, and I was warmly welcomed by two parishioners who were busy cleaning, but kindly paused to give me a history of the building and the churchyard.

In the north porch a life-sized medieval statue known as Cefyl Derfel (Derfel's horse) is said to represent a stag and was reputedly once positioned at the feet of a wooden image of St. Derfel, dressed in full warrior armour and carrying the wooden staff which shares its resting place.

In the middle age's pilgrims came to Llandderfel to pray to his image and to offer gifts for a blessing on their animals and for other favours. A legend foretold that the effigy would one day burn down a forest. In 1538 Thomas Cromwell's commissioner reported that five or six hundred pilgrims had made offerings on that year's feast day, Cromwell ordered it to be taken to London and used to light the pyre of a Jesuit priest, Father John Forest, confessor of Catherine of Aragon, who was burned alive for denying the supremacy of King Henry VIII as head of the Church. According to contemporary reports the effigy was carried into the marketplace by eight men, with three executioners holding it in ropes, in the manner of a condemned criminal. Cefyl Derfel escaped the grisly proceedings though is now minus the head, having reportedly been decapitated in the 18th century on the orders of the rural dean.

Deep cuts in the sides of the old sandstone doorway reminded me of those at Shotwick church which were the result of the action of sharpening of arrows, these however have been suggested to represent the flames destroying the image of Derfel.

Henry Robertson, the railway engineer who, among his many other achievements, built the viaducts at Cefn and Chirk and

the second chain bridge at Llangollen is buried here having died at Palé Hall, which he had built on the site of the previous hall, when he wasn't busy in his stints as MP for Shropshire and Merioneth.

When Trevor Fishlock visited the area, winkling out stories for his excellent Wild Tracks series, he stood on a hill behind Palé Hall and, while admiring the magnificent view over the Penllyn Valley, told how that vista was almost lost. A plan hatched in the 1890s to dam the Dee, would have flooded the valley to create a reservoir 24 miles long to supply London with water. A local vicar is reported as having said it would be an 'honorable sacrifice for Bala'. That plan was abandoned. There were similar plans to build two dams in the Ceiriog Valley in the 1920s, to supply Warrington with water. Lloyd George delivered a passionate speech against the drowning of 'his little piece of heaven' but it was ultimately lack of money which stopped the valleys being emptied of their people, to be filled with the gift from God.

Back in the village, he told how in an

Cefyl Derfel at Llandderfel Church

election in 1859, the local landowner, Sir Watkin Williams-Wynn (the 6th Baronet) expected his tenant farmers to vote his way. Many did not, five were ejected and the rent of sixteen others was raised. A plaque salutes three of the farmer families, one of those commemorated is Mary Jones, whose son Michael D. Jones will be further mentioned later. The old estate bonds were beginning to loosen, the Bala area would be a centre of political as well as religious protest.

Once again footpaths and the Dee are comparative strangers on the upstream stretch towards Bala. The road is more compliant, hugging the river through gentle, rolling, tree topped hills. As I left the Berwyn mountains, and the cosy settlements at their feet, I reflected on how much I had enjoyed this area. The legend-chaired tops, wild, isolated, bare, and windswept, which have long been a barrier to invaders and estate agents, a golden triangle of historic religious sites, the high hill of Moel Tŷ Uchaf with its circle of stones arranged by our ancestors, the Romany camp at Llandrillo, stories of UFO's in the hills. I suspected the Dee would have some surprises in store for me, but this area surpassed all expectations. There is magic here, there is also quirkiness, as I followed the road, a tree overhanging a bend had three brassieres hanging from it, like bawdy prayer flags, or possibly as an intergalactically recognised sign that it was safe for the aliens to return. And return I hopefully will, to walk the wild quiet places, maybe find a hidden valley where refuge can be found from the helter-skelter of the twenty first century.

From Llanfor, a hamlet which is said to have been more important than Bala in Tudor times, I walked out across the fields from the beautiful stone farm buildings and church. My map showed the path continuing the other side of the river, but my hopes of a fording were dashed, the flow was too strong. I heard a tractor on a hillside, and saw it being used to move boulders to the sides of a field, clearing the stones from the places where the forces of nature arranged them. So many demands on the land, increasing population, more mouths to feed, more places to live required, more services to be provided. Bio-fuel crops, solar panel farms. As Mark Twain said, "Buy land, they're not making it anymore".

11. Dwr – Water – A gift from God?

Where the Dee exits Llyn Tegid, I crossed another border, into the Snowdonia National Park, Lle i enaid gael llonydd – a place for the soul to have calm/peace. In previous times, it was not always so peaceful here, partly hidden within trees and shrubs, in the garden of Pen y Bont cottage, a flag flew high within the greenery, from a pole on the remains of the motte of Castell Gronw. This is a significant point, the castle would have controlled access over the Dee at the outlet of the lake, from which Y Bala takes its name. Close by, just north of the church at Llanfor, massive earthwork ramparts are thought to be the remains of another medieval castle. Llanfor's strategic importance goes back even further, aerial reconnaissance in the 1970s discovered an extensive Roman military complex to the south west of the current settlement. In Bala itself, we shall shortly arrive at Tomen y Bala. These structures were all built to restrict the movement of people through the lands, at the head of the lake.

Following the English conquest, this part of the Dee valley was said to have been difficult to control, in 1310 a borough was established at Bala 'for the king's benefit, for the security of those parts and to restrain the malice of evildoers and robbers in the locality.'

The old bridge has a pleasingly undulating wall, rising over an accumulation of dry stones where once there was water. It is now claimed by reeds, willow, and ash, the flow out of the lake having been diverted under a newer more streamlined bridge. I dawdled a while, doing the river version of gongoozling, looking downstream I noticed tail skippering circular splashes and flashes of silver fish and the lazy quivering of green water weed in the peat rich waters. I heard a scratchy bird call at the water's edge, a Heron flew lazily overhead. The morning rain had stopped, though the heavy dark grey cloud remained. As I gazed into the waters, I noticed that the flow was going back under the bridge, that is *upstream* into the lake. Another stunt to add to the repertoire of the tricks performed by the waters of the Holy river which already included flowing beneath the riverbed and 127 feet above it.

The search for Mabon ap Modron
The Eagle brought them to Llyn Llyw
(Llyn Tegid*) where the wise Salmon said
he would tell them what he knew, then
went up and down the river until at a
bend near Caer Loyw** (Caer Llion Fawr
– Chester*) *he heard such distress as he*
had never heard before. He invited Cei and
Gwrhir to ride upon his shoulders and
they journeyed until they came to a wall.
From the other side, they could hear
wailing and lamentations from a person,
saying no imprisonment was as grievous
as his. Mabon had been imprisoned from
birth and told them he could only be
released if someone fought for him.

Arthur summoned his warriors and
went to Caer Loyw, Mabon was freed, the
twenty- sixth of Culhwch's tasks had been
completed.
(* See earlier note re the Mabinogion)
**Caerloyw is the Welsh name for
Gloucester – on the River Severn.

Ahead of me on the lakeside path, I saw a flame raising, I heard shouts and cheers. My mother-in-law used to call her rarely used television set the idiot lantern, but the terminology is also apt for Chinese lanterns. A flickering flame carried it up before it fell in the trees just south of the campsite I was staying at, to who knows what effect. I followed the riverside path away from the bridge, stopping to enquire if an angler who was stood on the opposite bank, had had any luck. He was positioned where the former flow of the river, where Telford's control sluices operated, curves into the new line of the Dee. He flicked out his lure and told me he had caught a small perch earlier; but has previously caught pike here. I said it was unusual to see a river flow... backwards 'the gates must be closed' came the reply.

The path follows an embankment, an old map which I have notes that this area, and the land north of the Tryweryn is "liable to flooding". This is a reworked landscape; flows have been altered and defences put in place many times at this gathering point for the large volumes of the sometimes-tempestuous waters of southern Snowdonia. They are sent on their way down the Dee to be released into her estuary, into the sea, and to return, in the fullness of time through the clouds, back to the mountains. This area is a control point for water as well as people, the quiet Dee is joined by the noisy Tryweryn tumbling down through several weirs, where she is measured, metered, and guided onwards.

The main flow is under the old redundant railway bridge of the line to Ffestiniog, where a hunched grey heron waited for his supper, like a customer at a sushi bar. The mountain tops were chopped off by mist, I had a sudden feeling of well-being. Work was slipping away from my mind at the start of a two-week summer break, with rivers and mountains ahead of me, and strength in my legs. I followed the Tryweryn to the four arched stone fastness of Pont y Bala. A cut-out in the bank here looks like an emergency lay-by where canoeists can egress before they are swept into the tumbling weirs of the Dee Regulation System, of which this area plays a pivotal role and the workings of which I shall attempt in a very small way to give an overview as follows.

Llyn Tegid, the fair lake, is the largest in Wales, around four miles long, up to a mile wide and 150 feet deep. As we saw earlier, in the early 1800s William Jessop and Thomas Telford constructed sluices which raised the level to conserve water and regulate the flow of the Dee, to give a continuous water supply for the new Ellesmere Canal.

These sluices would remain in place until the 1950s when they were bypassed as part of the Bala Lake Scheme which would lower the lake outlet and install new sluice gates a short distance downstream. The scheme would store a large body of water in Llyn Tegid to support continuous abstraction from the Dee and reduce flooding in the Dee Valley downstream of Bala.

It would involve the construction of the new road bridge to accommodate a straightened deeper channel for the Dee, hence the high and dry old bridge. The Tryweryn would similarly be straightened with a flood channel broadly taking its old course, and two new channels utilising the existing flood arches under the railway line which would also be deepened and strengthened. The new channels would flow into a stilling basin from which the flow could be allowed to continue downstream or, by closing the new control sluices, (the 'gates' as described by the

1. *The tamed Tryweryn;*
2. *Llyn Tegid controllable, sometimes*

The Holy Dee   189

fisherman) to be diverted into Llyn Tegid, for use when required further downstream, hence a river flowing upstream.

The 'catchment waters' of the Dee have long been coveted, to quote J.S. Howson 'Were it not for the great reservoir of Bala Lake, the Dee would be almost dry in some seasons...just sparkling in a scanty stream over pebbles...Thus the need of giving an adequate water-supply to our great and growing towns in Cheshire and Lancashire....by building a breakwater a few feet high at the narrow end of the lake, so as slightly to raise its general surface by damming up a few mountain-passes where the land is of little value, so as in dry summers to store up the water still further in artificial lakes, and by 'impounding' the tributary called the Tryweryn, which enters the Dee just below Bala Lake, and which has a very extensive drainage area, – by these methods it has been calculated that both Liverpool and Manchester might receive a steady supply of water, for all future years, from the Meirionethshire hills. These facts or theories are of extreme interest; and the time may soon come when they will be made the subject of renewed consideration'.

Renewed consideration led to Llyn Celyn reservoir being constructed in the 1960s from which water is released into the Tryweryn, most of it passing through a four MW Hydro-electric station, to help maintain the flow in the Dee so that drinking water can be abstracted further downstream, including at Huntington water treatment works near Chester, which supplies water to Liverpool and the Wirral.

Other works in the Dee catchment area included the building of the Alwen reservoir, which was completed in 1921, initially to provide Birkenhead, but nowadays north-east Wales, with a direct gravity-fed supply as we saw earlier (Hence a tunnel carrying the headwaters of the Dee beneath itself further downstream) and the building of Llyn Brenig reservoir in the 1970s to further increase Dee abstraction via supply through the Alwen tributary.

The Dee Regulation Scheme collects data from many sources, one of the most important monitoring points is at Manley Hall weir, which we also passed earlier and is on a section of the river where flow can be readily measured after the boisterous flows down the valleys and above the flat stretch that meanders into Cheshire. This data allows appropriate and timely water releases to be made from the reservoirs, during low flows. It can take almost two days to reach the major abstraction points near Chester. There are seven major abstraction points, located in both England and Wales, used by three statutory water supply undertakings as well as the canal and river Trust. Also affected are leisure pursuits such as the National Whitewater Centre which relies on adequate water levels in the Tryweryn below the Celyn reservoir. Economics must also be added to the mix, gravity fed water being cheaper than pumped water, while the income provided by the electricity from the Hydro-electric generation will vary according to its value to users. The scheme supplies clean drinking water to some three million people, reduces flooding, safeguards the passage of migratory fish such as salmon, gives more control over pollution incidents, and the salinity of the river as well as providing recreational use and clean power generation, it maintains a balance between many interests and is an internationally recognised example of advanced river basin management.

How Llyn Celyn, which plays a crucial part in the scheme, came into being, is a rather less edifying story. Following my tip-off at Llandderfel, I decided to leapfrog upstream to take the opportunity provided by the dry summer and its lowering of the level of the reservoir.

I arrived at Llyn Celyn in the continuing mist of the previous day, stopping at a roadside plaque, I expected it to give a history of the village and the building of the reservoir. It commemorated Hafod Fadog, a farmstead which was used by Quakers for meetings and burials, and now lies beneath the waters, and goes on to say how many of the Quakers who emigrated to Pennsylvania, to find freedom of worship, came from this valley. They included the great-grandmother of Abraham Lincoln.

At each lay-by adjacent to the reservoir, I searched in vain for an interpretation board or plaque. Looking across the low-level waters, I could now make out the gentle gradient of the old railway line on the opposite shore. It wasn't until I reached the stopping point furthest up the valley and walked down an un-signposted lane, lined with moss and ferns that I saw a stone building with a cross on top which

I presumed to be a chapel. Immediately before the building is a neat memorial garden lined on two sides with headstones. Through a crazed and misted window, I could see a lectern and a small vase of flowers on the stone flagged floor, there were no chairs. The memorial is in Welsh only, reflecting the monoglot community who were displaced from here. It commemorates Capel Celyn as having been built in 1820 and pulled down in 1964 when the reservoir was built.

A rough stone path led down from the memorial building to the reservoir which as my friend had reliably informed me was at an exceptionally low level. I could see a raised stone covered area surrounded by the semi-ordered remains of a stone wall with the tree stumps of old hedge lines leading away into the mud. I wondered which building would have been on this spot, which would soon be covered once more by the water flowing down the Afon Celyn from the mist shrouded hills.

The stone path soon turned to mud, I followed the footsteps of previous visitors, which turned out to be a bad decision, I quickly sank in, almost to the top of my wellingtons. I looked ahead and saw that the footsteps stopped, not only that, but I could make out the top few inches of a green wellington, and close by, its accompanying partner, with the top just visible. I paused, I had little choice. Then it hit me, I really should not be here. Ordinarily the water level would be well above my head. Historically, this was once the centre of a small rural community

where families walked and talked and worked and played. It was creepy being in that spot, the mist added to my unease. I performed an ungainly retreat out of the quagmire, as quickly and quietly as I could.

The flooding of the valley was a hugely significant and controversial event for 20th century Wales, the language and culture of which was under growing pressure. The loss of the chapel and its cemetery was particularly offensive to the people of Capel Celyn and rural Wales. Some of the stones from the chapel have been used in the memorial chapel.

Authority for the reservoir was gained through an act of parliament, avoiding the need for consent from the Welsh planning authorities. Thirty-five of the thirty-six Welsh members of parliament opposed the bill, with one abstention. The official opening of the reservoir took place in October 1965, the ceremony lasting only a few minutes as protesters had cut the microphone wires and the chants of hundreds of others made the speeches inaudible. In October 2005, Liverpool City Council issued a public apology 'for any insensitivity by our predecessor council at that time'.

In a TV program presented by Huw Stephens the DJ, and son of Meic Stephens who painted the original and iconic "Cofiwch Dryweryn" graffiti on a roadside wall near Aberystwyth, he interviewed a lady who had attended the village school at Capel Celyn. She showed a photograph of her class, with a board behind them identifying them as "Disgyblion olaf Ysgol Celyn" – the last pupils of Ysgol Celyn. Another photo showed the skeleton walls of the roofless schoolhouse. She described how once a building became empty, it was demolished, and the stones from which they were built would be carried down the valley to be used in the dam on which they were sat. On my way there I had wondered what I would see, I was half expecting to see the remains of buildings, but this explained why there were none. She, like many others, now avoid Llyn Celyn if they can, preferring to use back roads. R.S. Thomas wrote:

There are places in Wales I don't go:
Reservoirs that are the subconscious
Of a people, troubled far down
With gravestones, chapels, villages even.

Llyn Celyn

12. Bala – a nonconformist town

I took an early Sunday morning stroll around Bala, picking out various points on the town trail leaflet. I started at the top of the high street where Ysgol Tŷ Dan Domen, the old grammar school, was founded in 1713 and offered a vigorous education, producing many outstanding academics and religious leaders.

On Heol y Domen, a light shone from on high through the moody grey mist, the voice of the preacher in the Capel Yr Annibynwyr (Congregational Chapel) carried out to the pavement, where I listened a while before dodging a polystyrene tray of discarded chips. The leaflet informed me that an earlier chapel and college were located opposite, and that Michael D Jones (son of Mary Jones of Llandderfel) was a minister here, he also became principal of the Methodist College (Calvinistic) which was opened in 1867 by Lewis Edwards to prepare men for the ministry and is now Coleg y Bala, the Youth Centre of the Presbyterian Church of Wales. During Michael D. Jones's principalship, a row broke out between two rival factions within Welsh congregationalism over its constitution, which led to a split and for a period the Congregationalists had two seminaries in Bala. This was not the only religious falling out in Bala, in the 1740s Howell Harris the Methodist reformer was almost killed by an angry mob, while in 1793 another Methodist preacher was attacked in a house opposite Ye Old Bulls head which was led by the vicar of Llanycil. Emotions can run strong in Y Bala, as if they are whipped up by the storms that run across Llyn Tegid.

The current Capel Tegid was built in 1866 in ambitious gothic style to seat a thousand people, at that time, the population of Bala was around 1,500. This chapel has made an immense contribution to Welsh culture and faith, in front stands the statue of Thomas Charles the Methodist minister, writer and publisher and a pioneer of the Sunday school system in Wales. The map on the leaflet is marked with a further chapel as well as English, Anglican, and Catholic churches, and a religious college. I came across numerous plaques and statues, even gateposts with religious symbols, the first town on the Holy Dee has religion ingrained in its very stones. From here the waters are collected from the mountain fastnesses around and sent on their way, through valley and plain to Chester, the book-end Holy city.

The wide high street was originally built to accommodate fairs and markets. Today it is not quite wide enough to accommodate the large pick-up vehicles which jut out from their angled parking places into the carriageway. No need for speed bumps here to slow the traffic. Cars accessing the petrol station at a busy junction add to the smiling soft chaos of the traffic flow, if it were to be recorded to a soundtrack of experimental jazz, it would make a great art film, which could be shown at the nearby Buddug cinema, a plaque on the wall of which commemorates Cerdd Dant, the art of performing poetry to harp accompaniment. On my visit the advertised feature was for Transylvania 3, Welsh films are also shown.

On another visit, I arrived at Y Tomen in the evening and followed the delicious corkscrew path which leads up through a deceivingly long route to the top, which was sadly littered. The Tomen or motte,

constructed by the Normans is nine metres high, one of the highest in Wales, an interpretation board showed a much less cluttered view from the top in 1781 from Thomas Pennants "The journey to Snowden". Pennant wrote that Bala was noted for its vast trade in woolen stockings 'during winter the females, through love of society, often assemble at one another's houses to knit, sit around a fire and listen to some old tale, some ancient song, or the sound of a harp. This is called cymorth gwau or the knitting assembly'. The stockings are said to have become popular after George III said they were the only ones which relieved his rheumatism.

I made my way to the Royal White Lion Hotel where George Borrow stayed in 1854 and found myself a seat next to the fireplace which I like to think is the one where he sat and had his discussion with the Wolverhampton gent 'on the spree' and the more agreeable Doctor. There was no freckled maid on my visit and the piped music was a modern addition from Borrow's days. After a stormy night, Borrow went on to fuel another of his mammoth walks by enjoying a breakfast of "pot of hare; ditto of trout; pot of prepared shrimps; dish of plain shrimps; tin of sardines; beautiful beef-steak; eggs; muffin; large loaf, and butter, not forgetting capital tea"! I noticed full English breakfasts and a 'go large' option was available on their menu, surely there is a marketing opportunity here for a further 'Go Borrow' option for those who don't want to eat anything else for a few days?

Returning to the lake I saw the *Loch* Café and for a moment the name made me wonder if I had taken a serious wrong turn. There was no blazing sunset to photograph, the lower hills were visible through the shrouding grey mist but Yr Aran and Cader Idris were hidden. Midges aplenty accompanied me as I walked, a few bats made valiant attempts to relieve my plight, but were outnumbered. Passing the building on the foreshore which houses the lake warden etc. I was reminded of a photo I had seen of Atlantic sized waves humbling this building, I considered the deep body of water out there and how the wind funnelling down the valley would scoop it up to pound its shores.

There are several legends associated with the birth of Llyn Tegid, one tells of how there was a sacred well which had a goddess who insisted that a lid was put in place at each nightfall. A guardian of the well was given the task, but after a boozy night, he forgot to put the lid on, flooding the old town which now lies beneath the lake. Another legend concerns Tegid Foel a wicked prince who ruled the town. To celebrate the birth of his grandson he invited many guests including the best harpist in Wales. As the harpist was playing, he kept hearing a voice, quiet at first then more insistent saying "Vengeance will come!" He saw a small bird watching him and realised it was the bird speaking. The bird left the palace, signalling the harpist to follow him up a high hill overlooking the town. The bird sang to the harpist who fell asleep. When he awoke, he saw the palace and the town had been completely submerged by water.

Back on Pont Mwnwgl-y-llyn, the bridge at the neck of the lake, the last of the natural light allowed me to pick out the river weeds trailing downstream, normal service had been resumed. I completed my walk to the lovely campsite tucked away in the darkness of the trees at the side of the lake, there was perfect peace just inside the Snowdonia national Park.

I retraced my steps along the foreshore in the morning, dropping down onto the paths through the reeds from where I noticed the strandline of washed-up material was just inches below the top of the flood embankment. Reed buntings flew up from adjacent to path and hung off the stalks.

All manner of craft was taking to the water, sailing dinghies, paddle boards, surf boards, kayaks, canoes, as well as swimmers. A feast of technicolour orange and bright blues in front of the grey steel water and sky. Soggy youngsters squealed and huddled for warmth, laughing, eating their packed lunches while ducks reclaimed the vacated lakeside. As I sat on a bench on the embankment observing the upper end of the lake and its surrounding peaks which had varying amounts of grey mist which never quite cleared, I began to wonder if there is a shade of paint called "Bala Grey".

About a mile south of Bala alongside the A494 at the side of the lake, sits the church of Llanycil which is built on an ancient Celtic Christian site. The church was declared redundant in 2003 but was rescued and converted into 'Mary Jones World'. Mary Jones at the age of nine

Sculpture at Pen y Bont campsite

1. Reed Bunting; 2. Fade to grey

decided she wanted a bible in her own language, she saved for six years and in 1800 walked 25 miles barefooted from Llanfihangel-y-pennant to Bala to buy one from the Reverend Thomas Charles. The centre is run by the Bible Society which was formed in part from hearing her story and seeing her devotion.

I visited in early autumn, the berries on the yew trees were vibrant red, the sun highlighted a rising curve of headstones. Thomas Charles is laid to rest here, J.S. Howson wrote 'It is not to be expected that an English Churchman can write with enthusiasm on the Annals on Nonconconformity' but went on to describe Charles of Bala as 'an eminently wise and laborious, as well as godly and devoted man'. It is now possible to follow the 'Mary Jones Walk' which can be finished at the centre and is based on the route she is likely to have taken to Bala. I met a group of boy scouts at Llanuwchllyn who were walking the trail in the opposite direction.

The Bala lake railway runs through four and a half miles alongside the eastern edge of the lake on the bed of the old Ruabon to Barmouth line. This is the second resurrected section of the line that we have come across, though this one is narrow gauge, built by dedicated individuals using redundant equipment from slate quarries in North Wales, another story of a vision made real by the hard graft of many people over long years, and it may not be over, there are plans to extend the line to Bala town. I have a recurring thought that if the entire line were still in existence, we could hop on a train near our home and travel along this amazing route to Barmouth.

I embarked at Llanuwchllyn joined by Sophia under the growling mist covered Aran's. The raw power of steam pulled us out of the station through osier, oak, ash, hazel, and red berried rowans, Welsh blacks lumbered in a boulder cleared field, white horses chased canoeists on the lake, a ram raced alongside the train past spreading lustrous ferns and thick luxuriant moss, gorse, and bilberry. The wind whipped up, propelling dinghies along the water surface, a heron stood at the edge her black crest flapping as she quickly realigned her death stare. Streams fizzed below the tracks draining the sodden hills into the lake. Throughout the journey the smiles of the driver and his assistant shouted out 'job satisfaction'! Orange sailed windsurfers slid across the surface of the slate grey lake, a fog of steam swept past us, there was the smell of sulphur, soot was in the air, a fire and brimstone elemental journey. On the opposite bank we could see the Glan-llyn outdoor centre, which is run by the Urdd to provide opportunities through the medium of Welsh to develop the skills of young people to make a positive contribution in their communities. When Plas Glan-llyn became available at the end of the 1940s, Sir Ifan ab Owen Edwards established it as an Urdd centre, a welcome egalitarian re-assignment. Previously it had been used as a hunting lodge by the Williams-Wynn family, who in the time of the fourth and fifth baronets claimed absolute fishing rights on the lake, banning fishing with nets and forbidding boats except by their permission, which they granted only to other gentlemen.

Back at Llanuwchllyn, we halted next to the running shed, from where the smell of hot oil emanated and shining brass magically rises out of rust. Welsh liquid sunshine fell from the heavens, an atmospheric end to the journey.

On a subsequent, blistering August bank holiday I drove through Llangower, through the smell of summer barbecues, and the sound of water splashing, shrieking, laughter, and dog-barking, stopping once more at Llanuwchllyn

station for a cooling ice cream, when I noticed a fund-raising sign 'Driver for a fiver'! I defy anyone with an ounce of childhood remaining pure within them to resist such a sign. I climbed aboard the 'Maid Marion' and was given a 'crash course' in steam train driving which finished with the advice that 'any fool can drive one, but it takes a special kind of fool to stop one'! I gave a toot of steam and operated valves and levers in a guided sequence to propel the fire breathing beast up and down the tracks. I've sometimes wondered what drives the volunteers and enthusiasts who restore and maintain these lines, to give up their spare time and sometimes travel long distances to put in the hard graft in all weathers to make these things happen. Now I know, mere words cannot convey how good it felt to drive a steam train a short distance and back again.

Llyn Tegid Railway

13. Llanuwchllyn - Exodus

Llanuwchllyn, the parish above the lake, the first settlement to lie on the Dee, which I would visit last, a small community whose patriotic sons have played an incredibly significant role in Wales' history.

Michael D. Jones, who we have already met at Llandderfel and Bala, was a minister and teacher, he also played a prominent part in the foundation of the Welsh colony in Patagonia which he was driven to do partly by the spirit of nationalism, and partly by the radicalism bred in him on account of the oppression of the Tory landlords in Wales. The 'Welsh Not' was commonly used in schools in the 19th century, it would have been put around the neck of any child caught speaking Welsh who was then compelled to seek out another language transgressor and pass it on. The child in its possession at the end of the day or week was punished. It was introduced after the Welsh language had been diagnosed as a kind of 'sickness' with the publication of an 1847 report into the state of Welsh education, commonly known as the blue books. It concluded that the Welsh language was the cause of stupidity, promiscuity, and unruly behaviour. The Mimosa set from Liverpool in 1865 to establish Y Wladfa in Patagonia. Around 50,000 Patagonians are of Welsh descent, with *yr hen iaith* continuing to be spoken by some 5,000 people.

Owen M. Edwards was a writer and lecturer who became the chief inspector of schools for Wales, while his son Sir Ifan ap Owen Edwards, founded Urdd Gobaith Cymru. The first camp was held in his garden at Neuadd Wen, before it was moved to the larger site at Glan-llyn.

I walked into the grounds of Eglwys Deiniol Sant which sits atmospherically within its stone walls, cheek by jowl with Yr Eagles public house. George Borrow could not attend church on the morning of his stay at Bala as there was no service, I wondered if it might be here (alternatively it may have have been Llanycil) where he attended a 'low, long ancient edifice' and heard an 'excellent sermon', which was delivered in Welsh. I was hoping to take a look around, possibly to find some record confirming his visit, but also simply because I enjoy infusing myself with the quiet, soothing and uplifting sense of the sacred that these places always bring, but sadly found it closed, the doorway blocked off. A later enquiry however, was heartening in that I found reports of plans announced to mark the 150 years since the Mimosa's voyage to Patagonia, to restore the church into a new heritage and visitor centre, bringing the Grade II listed building back into community use. It will have an exhibition space recognising local figures, including Michael D. Jones.

My campsite was set pleasingly next to the Afon Lliw, overlooked by majestic mount Aran. I spent the next day cycling around the lanes at the top of the lake, sometimes leaving my bike tucked behind hedges before continuing on foot along marshy paths. I came back to my bike in the corner of one field to find it surrounded by cows, who were insistent it was now their bike, not mine. I had to make a retreat and return later when they had become bored of it.

When I arrived at the shoreline at Llangower, the crowds had mostly left, the last big group formed a caravan along the

Owen Morgan Edwards and Sir Ifan ab Owen Edwards

strandline, walking towards the car park carrying outsize bags and fold away chairs followed by reluctant children. A small group of men sat cross legged under the trees around a shisha pipe talking gently, their laughter as warm and soft as the last rays of the sun which was dipping towards Arenig Fawr. I stripped off in a quiet spot amongst the trees and left my clothes, on a shingle spit where the Afon Glyn winds into the Tegid and waded out to join the rare Gwyniad, a fish left behind at the end of the last ice age and unique to Llyn Tegid, hopefully not giving them the biggest shock, they've had in the last 10,000 years. I swilled the waters over my head and shoulders, it felt very satisfying even though by some accounts, I was not in the waters of the Dee, which are confined to their own exclusive route, within the bosom of the lake. Michael Drayton, wrote in Poly-Olbion:

'So, Lavern and the Lue, themselves that head-long throwe
Into the spacious Lake, where Dee unmixt doth flowe'

George Borrow recounted a druidical legend, 'The Dee springs from two mountains high up in Merionethshire, called Dwy Fawr and Dwy Fach...whose waters pass through those of the lake of Bala without mingling with them'

A final trick performed by the Holy river which in the rarefied air of the mountains and following on from her earlier achievements, now seems to me to be completely feasible. My dip was unbeatable, better than any luxury spa, bathing in the cool waters, breathing in the crisp alpine air was an elemental experience. I soon dried off in the late sun and gentle breeze, re-dressed and cycled up a hill at the southern tip of the lake to catch the exultant sun set above where the Dee enters the lake and is shaken but not stirred.

I cycled back slowly, pausing to see herons returning to their high-level roost behind a field of drying hay, I pedalled slower and slower, for this was an evening to squeeze every ounce of joy out of. In Llanuwchllyn I toasted my good fortune with a delicious pint in front of the pub-shop cabinet with its Paxo and Fray Bentos tinned pies and toothpaste, in a swirl of 'hwyl'. I savoured my time in the most westerly settlement of my journey where the Celtic language and traditions are at

their strongest, still holding fast. Gildas the wise, the sixth century British monk who emigrated to Brittany wrote "The barbarians drive us to the sea; the sea throws us back on the barbarians: thus two modes of death await us, we are either slain or drowned". I pushed my bike back to the campsite, I couldn't possibly ride it because by now my gaze was constantly drawn to the enormity of the star-filled sky, which I was able to fully drink in from a chair, beside my old campervan, well into the quiet night beside the Afon Lliw which passed quietly on its way to meet the Dee.

I took an early morning walk along the river, her waters were clear at the edge,

1. A likely swimming spot; 2. Sunset over the Dee entering Llyn Tegid

graduating to the colour of cold tea and almost black in the deep of the far bank. Spidery pond skaters, twitched on the surface, skirting over the flow. Just downstream the water's edge appeared to be receiving rain they were so numerous. A trout in search of breakfast leapt and belly flopped. A pair of dippers engaged in an acrobatic dog fight came in and out of shafts of low sunlight, their calls of a higher pitch than their downstream cousins. A rivulet flowed next to my pitch, a tributary of a tributary of the Dee which

The Holy Dee 205

though tiny, had a line of leaflitter, twigs and reeds caught up in a fence about three feet above its current placid level. A campsite notice advised this area can sometimes flood. My map showed a myriad of thin blue lines in this area. The Lliw and the Twrch, join the Dee on the alluvial flats of the lacustrine delta shortly before they enter the lake, while the Llafar and the Glyn as well as numerous other watercourses flow directly into Llyn Tegid.

I followed the fish-darting, Heroned and forded Lliw up the valley, passing a spot where the stones of the river are formed into a weir on the downstream side of a road bridge, holding back the flow, a useful sheep wash. As I progressed up the valley, I noticed fields cleared of stones, some larger ones remaining where the forces of nature deposited them. And then as I cycled along with my head in the clouds, I saw a circular arrangement of stones on a hill above the road which stopped me in my tracks, I took out both my maps of this area but neither showed them, in my mind I begin to make all sorts of alignments with solstices and peaks, I learnt later that a farmer had arranged them so, nevertheless a fabulous aesthetic sight and an enjoyable diversion.

I stopped at an attractive old building to read a plaque, which read 'these alms houses were erected in 1721 for the shelter of three decayed old men and three old women'. Continuing up the valley I passed many gorgeous rowan trees, the mountain ash, the lady of the mountains, bright red berried, which brought colour and provided havens for birds. From close to an abandoned stone house, I could see the summit of the steep rocky slopes to my left topped by the dilapidated ruins of Castell Carndochan, the reason for its location being immediately apparent.

Despite the absence of defenders who could rain down rocks, pointed weapons and lord knows what else, there was no way I was ascending from this direction. My map showed a track leading over the shoulder of the hill amidst the gentler contour lines to the south west of the top. As I walked up the track, the views were incredible, swathes of green trees giving way to brown heather slopes, which in turn led to the peaks of Arenig Fawr.

Leaving the track, I engaged in what is for me, a rare process. In the previous

Views from Castell Carndochan

days, my energy level had dipped, so, rather than choosing the most direct route to the summit, which would inevitably lead to retreats and diversions around boggy areas and dead ends, I paused and surveyed a route. I could see the outline of a sheep at the top, jutting out majestically, an ovine declaration of the current ownership of the stones, leading up to her there were fleeting thin tracks, which I set off to follow. Where they fizzled out, I paused again, selecting the route which would need least energy. It wasn't the north face of the Eiger, but for my more modest challenge, I found it an effective, almost meditative walk to the top,

avoiding the soaking heavy mosses, which, the experience of previous walks has given me, retain their ample water content long after the skies have filled them. As I slumped onto a suitable stone to sit on at the top, my thoughts returned to the alms house and decay. A pair of Buzzards rose from below, flapping, gliding, flashing brown and white, exemplars of energy conservation.

Walking through the remaining low grey walls, and the bases of towers and doorways, I could now see the waters of Llyn Tegid, a blue-grey ribbon following the fault line to the north-east. Squeaking House Martins darted close to me, feeding

on insects carried up on the wind.

Castell Carndochan is thought to have been built by Llywelyn ap Iorwerth in the 13th century. Little is known of its history, from construction through to abandonment. It would originally have consisted of four towers and a surrounding wall which the centuries have collapsed into heaps of rubble. In the 1860s a 12-year-old shepherd boy noticed flecks of gold within some quartz found nearby. Gold was subsequently mined from the land below the castle until around 1905. Carndochan was the most easterly mine within the Merioneth gold bearing area, and despite being small, enough gold was mined here for the landowner Sir Watkin Williams-Wynn (the 6th Baronet) to have manufactured, what is thought to be the largest object to be made from Welsh gold. I hope that the shepherd boy was handsomely rewarded. The design of the Castell Carndochan gold cup and cover is based on the cup made in 1536 for Henry VIII for his third wife Jane Seymour. It is inscribed with several family mottoes including eryr eryrod eryri ('the eagle of the eagles of Snowdonia').

From my lofty viewpoint I looked down at where the buildings for the gold

Sign outside the Wynnstay Arms in Ruabon village which was the former seat of the Williams-Wynn family

mine stood and thought of how the gold cup, formed out of the spoils of the hill, was won by the sweat of the miners. The words of the hymn Calon Lan, came into my head,

Nid wy'n gofyn bywyd moethus,
Aur y byd na'i berlau mân:
Gofyn wyf am galon hapus,
Calon onest, calon lân.

I do not ask for a luxurious life
the world's gold or its fine pearls,
I ask for a happy heart,
an honest heart, a pure heart.

The view ahead of me, and the freedom with which I had to enjoy it, was worth all the gold in the world. In the distance I could see Llanuwchllyn and thought of Michael D. Jones and the founding of Y Wladfa on the other side of the world. It must have been an unbelievable wrench to leave here in search of liberty.

I returned down the valley to follow footpaths through the fields to the site of Caer Gai an auxiliary Roman fort, capable of housing a garrison of more than 500 soldiers sited at a strategic point in the Roman road system, located on a spur overlooking the Dee just before she flows in to Llyn Tegid. My map also shows Roman settlements on the other side of the valley, while the recently discovered site at Llanfor shows a long period of activity in this area. The Romans were present along the full length of the Dee from its estuary through Chester to this point where she enters the valley. The rectangular earthworks of the site which is thought to have been occupied until the mid-second century are clearly visible. Archaeological surveys have revealed buried features here including a possible bathhouse. Today the stone topped earthworks provide shelter for cows.

14. To the source

Mindful that the best days of summer lay behind me, I pushed on to the source. The Dee was surprisingly full and fast flowing through the meadows above Llyn Tegid from where its way weaved up the valley, criss-crossing under the road, at which I paused wherever I could, to see it go on its way. Several convoys of cars passed me, one consisted of old sportscars, a silver open top variant passed me at speed, then doubled back, before pulling up in a layby where the man in the passenger seat wrestled a map this way and that. They headed off again, in the original direction, the driver not looking confident in the skill of the map reader, they didn't seem to know where they were going, but wherever it was, they needed to be there fast.

I found an overgrown footpath to reacquaint me with the Dee, so overgrown in fact, that it is possible that it had not been walked in living memory. A watery route led me through overhanging trees, on a stone wall there were wonderful greens of mosses so deep that my hand could disappear right into them. I crossed the old railway track for the last time, it was time to say goodbye to the route of the Ruabon to Barmouth line which had been my, and the Dee's companion in the valley for over thirty miles.

I arrived at the alpine river as the sun showed itself through the clouds and made my way across one the highest crossing points on the Dee, via steppingstones only to pause to admire the view up to Aran Fawddwy. The high-water mark of twigs and reeds on the banks indicated that the stones would be likely to soon be submerged by the rising winter level.

I followed another overgrown path to a track above which my map showed a 'settlement', a notation far too interesting to bypass. The intermittent path through bogs and tussocks led me to the rough stone base of a former dwelling. There were no clues to its age, but whoever lived there had great views over the valley and down to Llyn Tegid.

I saw the Dee tumbling fast past an old stone building which had a doorway

Stepping-stones

opening directly onto the steep tumbling flow. A beautiful, peaceful, remote spot.

Returning to the forestry track, which was solid underfoot, was a welcome change from the ankle twisting danger of the bog and moss ground. The downside was that I find the enveloping regularity of conifer forests disorientating and had to keep checking my map to convince myself that I was going the right way, as the course of the track strayed from the route of the river. False summits and thin air topography eventually brought me to a ford, where the Dee crosses the track, this re-assured me that I was headed in the right direction. It was not the most direct route, I had to firmly repel any notion of taking a shortcut through the deceiving trees or the treacherous bogs.

The track dropped to a gate from which the landscape thankfully opened. To my left I could see the channel of the new-born Dee curving to the base of Dduallt's 662m (2172 feet) bulk which stood sheer-cliffed in front of me. The sun had already set behind her, she reminded me of Cwm Idwal with darker, presumably wetter sections of rock and deep chasms like those at the Devils Kitchen. I decided to head to the channel to follow the final

stages of the river but was soon persuaded to think again. I probed several routes, but they invariably consisted of deep moss and heather which were perfect at concealing yawning mud filled trenches. The bone white tree stumps were additional knee-jarring hazards. I retreated to the track which follows the perimeter of the forestry plantation leading closer to cliff, the wind rose, and the trees knocked together in applause of my foolhardiness.

The shorter route to the channel was little better, though I was heartened to see the footprints of another walker who had come the same way. I used my stick to probe my way, trying to pick out sturdy

tussocks of grass through the gorgeously multi-coloured deep mosses and heathers which tried to lull my senses and suck me down to the underworld. It occurred to me that the footprints I had seen were going one way only, so either my invisible co-walker had taken a different route back, or he was in the process of becoming the next Lindow Man. It was slow, exhausting progress but the cliffs were slowly drawing closer. I could see white flecks of sheep in impossibly high places. Eventually I arrived at the massive stone blocks at the base of the scree slope. I looked up and saw others, some precariously balanced, a living landscape, now would not be a good

time for an earth tremor. White clouds sped over the top of the cliffs.

I traced the flow to where the first rills and runnels of the fledgling Dee emanate at the foot of the cliff, where the first nourishing, cleansing droplets of the wizard stream are coalesced to be sent on their eventful near seventy-mile journey to the sea. Gradually the shape of a stone structure formed out of the jumble of fallen, perfectly camouflaged grey rocks, I was almost upon them before it became apparent. Could this be a shrine, or a pre-forestation, pre-marshy quagmire sheepfold?

The point where the Holy Dee arises from Mother Earth seems to me to be highly significant, even though I had it all to myself. I have no doubt that if, in a parallel reality, the Dee had been relocated to the Himalayas, I would have been surrounded by pilgrims drinking from its first pure drops while incantations carried on the wind into a swirl of prayer flags. At the Kumbh Mela on the mother Ganges, a hundred million Hindus bathe to cleanse

1. Nearing the source; 2. Dduallt; 3. The stone structure at the source

their sins, but here there is glorious solitude.

In Edmund Spenser's epic romantic poem, The Faerie Queene, this was the spot where Merlin delivered Arthure to Old Timon, for his long education ...

Unto old Timon he brought me bylive,
Old Timon, who in youthly years hath beene
In warlike feates th'expertest man alive,
And is the wisest now on earth I weene;
His dwelling in a valley greene,
Under the foot of Rauran mossy hore
From whence the river Dee as silver cleene,
His tombling billowes roll with gentle rore:

I reflected on the journey that had brought me to this spot, through wind and rain, sun, and snow, spread over several years. Happy, privileged memories whirled about in my head. I thought of the characters I had met, the places of worship I had visited and of man's effect on the river and its people, but it is the sum of all these parts, the interconnectedness of the entire river ecosystem which makes it complete, each tiny link in the chain of being that stretches back to Point of Ayr and Hilbre plays its part in the story, the cycle of life, the song of the Dee. A river whose time-defying waters connect the past with the present and will go on to sate our thirst, to feed our industries, to entertain and enrapt those whose path she crosses into the future, as long as we look after this precious home of ours.

I rested for some time at the assembly of stones and listened to the silence, there were no human sounds, no sign of human habitation in any direction. Bliss. A Raven cronked to break my reverie, at the western end of the cliff wall a kestrel hovered. I scattered some water, out of my bottle which I had filled from my tap at home that morning, as an offering, the water of the Dee returned to the Dee. I gave thanks to the nourishment it has provided me. Yes, this is a shrine. The wizard stream begins. Pilgrimage over.

Bibliography

Alan Godfrey Maps, (2002) *Old Ordnance Survey Maps Bala 1899*, Second edition 1901 Petersen Printers, Jarrow

Barrell John, (2013) *Edward Pugh of Ruthin*, The University of Wales Press, Cardiff.

CADW, (2016) *Llangollen: Understanding Urban Character*, Cardiff.

Daniel Westover (2011) *R.S. Thomas, a Stylistic Biography*, University of Wales Press, Cardiff.

David Crane and Gill Smith, (2019) *Myths and Legends of Llangollen and the Dee Valley*, Fineline Print and web, Ruthin.

Enjoy Medieval Denbighshire, (2012) published by Denbighshire County Council's Tourism Marketing Department.

Edmund Spenser, (1590) *The Faerie Queen*, London.

Forsyth Mark, (2016) *The Etymologicon*, Icon Books Ltd. London.

Graham Davies, (2007) *Real Wrexham*, Seren, Bridgend.

Gwyn Jones and Thomas Jones (1984) *The Mabinogion*, The Guernsey Press Co, Ltd, Guernsey.

John Davies, (1994) *A History of Wales*, Penguin Books Limited, London.

J.S. Howson and Alfred Rimmer, (1993) *The River Dee*, special edition, Library and Information Service, Cyngor Sir Clwyd, Mold.

Michael Drayton, (1612) *Poly-Olbion*.

Myrddin ap Dafydd, (2019) *The Welsh Marches from the West*, Gwasg Carreg Gwalch, Llanrwst.

Pennant, Thomas, (1998) *A tour in Wales*, abridged by David Kirk, Gwasg Carreg Gwalch, Llanrwst.

Peter Humphries, (2001) *On the trail of Turner in north and south Wales*, South western Printers, CADW Cardiff.

Richard J Turner-Thomas, (2005) *Pontcysyllte Aqueduct Restoration*, printed by Pensoft in Bulgaria.

Roy Wilding, (1997) *The Miller of Dee*, published by Gordon Emery, Chester.

Ruabon Parish Church, (1998) published by RJL Smith & Associates, Much Wenlock.

Simon Ward, (2013) *Chester a History*, The History Press, Stroud.

The Boat Museum Society, (2010) *Waterways Journal volume 12*, Nayler the Printers, Accrington.

Transactions of the Historic Society of Lancashire and Cheshire volume 32. (1880) Published by Adam Holden, Liverpool.

Y Geiriadur Mawr, (2010) *The Complete Welsh-English – English-Welsh Dictionary*, Dinefwr Press, Gomer, Llandybie.

COMPACT CYMRU

COMPACT CYMRU
– MORE TITLES:

www.carreg-gwalch.cymru

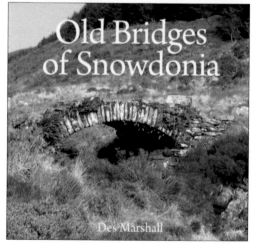